SACRED SPACES for INSPIRED LIVING

Your Guide to DESIGN ENLIGHTENMENT

"You must have a room or a certain hour of the day or so where you do not know what was in the morning paper...a place where you can simply experience and bring forth what you are and what you might be.....At first you may find nothing is happening, but if you have a sacred place and use it, take advantage of it, something will happen.

-JOSEPH CAMPBELL

SACRED SPACES *for* INSPIRED LIVING

by BEATRICE PILA-GONZALEZ

Balboa Press books may be ordered through booksellers or by contacting:

Balboa Press
A Division of Hay House
1663 Liberty Drive
Bloomington, IN 47403
www.balboapress.com
1 (877) 407-4847

Design, Layout & Illustrations by Gabriela Noelle Gonzalez

Sacred Spaces for Inspired Living: Your Guide to Design Enlightenment / Beatrice Pila-Gonzalez
p. cm.

ISBN: 978-1-5043-6420-1 (sc)
ISBN: 978-1-5043-6421-8 (e)

Library of Congress Control Number: 2016913808

HF0000.A0 A00 2010
299.000 00–dc22 2010999999

First Edition

Printed in China

Balboa Press rev. date: 09/22/2016

SACRED

Regarded with respect and reverence;
set apart and dedicated for some purpose or sentiment.

INSPIRED

Of extraordinary quality as if arising from some external force.
To influence, move, or guide by divine or supernatural.

ENLIGHTENED

Freed from ignorance and misinformation;
instructed and encouraged in moral, intellectual,
and spiritual improvement.

To my family for their constant belief in me and particularly to my mother who ignited my initial spark of design.

I am blessed with the most supportive and creative people surrounding me, more than any woman could ask for. To my husband, Carlos, and daughter, Gabi, who I am blessed to work with. I can't begin to express my love and gratitude for having both of you to share creation with every day.

Special thanks to Gabi for enhancing each written word with the graphics and layout to accompany them helping to make my vision easier and clearer to understand. I couldn't have done it without you.

FOREWORD

*T*hey say home is where the heart is.

But what if your heart has been hurt? What if your heart is heavy, busy, stressed out, frustrated?

What if your heart is overworked and overwhelmed? Is that then home?

In being on this journey of Design Enlightenment, I have come to learn about my own heart and how in many ways, home did not feel like home.

Before this process, I really didn't want to be at "home" because to be home meant to be in pain.

I grew up in a house where it was not uncommon to hear my father yelling at the top of his lungs about something.

A home where my stepmother's unhappiness brought on by my father's temper created a home where there were a lot of rules. Rules to try to create calm out of the chaos.

Home was where the unhappiness was, and later on as an adult it was reflected in my lifestyle. No wonder I spent most of my twenties bouncing from place to place with no furniture of my own and no long term plans to stay anywhere. As I eased into my professional life, I chose a job that required I live in corporate housing and move once every four months to a new city. Beautiful but sterile corporate housing and never in one place long enough to get "settled."

I had learned when you stayed in one place and it was called home, bad things happened. Better to be on the go. Better to be on the move.

Now here's the crazy thing. Prior to going through this process of Design Enlightenment, I had not fully identified this. I truly did not feel like anything was "wrong." There was no reason to think I didn't want to be home. I loved my life. To me, I was on an adventure! During those times, I was not unhappy or dissatisfied. I had the job of my dreams and a really phenomenal life. In so many ways, I had everything I had ever wanted. And that's the thing I became present to during this process. Everything I had ever wanted, but what about the things I didn't want? What about the things I thought I didn't need or were unnecessary? For example, I never ate at home. I always, always ate out. I knew I preferred to eat out versus eating in, but I thought, Who doesn't? It's more convenient, and you don't have to wash the dishes! Right?

Prior to this process, I really didn't want to buy a bunch of furniture, but I thought I was being practical. I mean, buying furniture takes time and costs money, and if you're not settled yet, isn't it wasteful? What if in a couple of years you won't need it anymore? It all made sense to me until I went through this process and realized I rarely ate dinner or lunch at home. I rarely had people over. I never sat on the couch and watched a movie. Never.

Why?

I had other things to do. Other things, not at home.

Home was not a place you did enjoyable things.

In going through this process, when I answered the questionnaire in chapter 1 that asked what pastime or memory from your childhood you remember most fondly, I was brought to tears realizing how few there were.

In fairness, I did have some. I loved reading. Sitting in a corner and getting lost in another world. TV was another great escape. I remember every summer as a little kid being in front of the TV at 10 a.m. ready to watch *The Price is Right*. And then playing with my little brother.

So I came to realize that as an adult, since I no longer watched TV, I could read anywhere and my brother was grown and gone, happiness could not be found at home. I had to go out — or so I unconsciously believed.

Today that's different. I don't need to go out for happiness. Happiness is sitting in my pink chair in my living room with a candle lit, having a great conversation with a friend or my brother who's visiting sitting across from me in the gorgeous gray leather and velvet chair I selected for the very purpose of being a conversation chair.

Happiness is sitting in the breakfast nook in the morning with my smoothie, looking out at the east views, the sky smiling at me while I answer e-mail and connect with the world.

Happiness is sitting on my gorgeous white couch snuggled up with a cup of tea watching all the movies from the eighties and nineties that I never saw.

Happiness is walking into a place and calling it home.

A home that is a place for living. Really living.

Soaking up each unappreciated but precious ritual of life.

Eating

Working

Sleeping

Relaxing

Bathing

These things we do every day but take for granted that make up 90 percent of our life.

Doesn't it make sense that the space that we do them in is sacred?

That it represents who we are to the core of our being?

This is what this book is about. **Uncovering who we really are at our core, bringing to the surface our deepest desires for living, and then providing a fun and magical journey to create a home that will bring all of that to life.**

In these next pages, you are in great hands. More than likely your situation is not as extreme as mine was. However, **if you have picked up this book you have a craving, as I did, to create a space that is sacred. A space that is inspiring. A space you can call home.** To do this, you have an amazing guide. Bea brings to these pages much more than thirty years of experience and countless awards and accolades. She brings to these pages a deep passion for everyone to have a sacred space. A passion for people and families to *live* together, intentionally, through design.

As you go through these pages, allow yourself to dream and create whatever you have longed for. Bea will provide the map; you simply need to take the steps. And step by step, as you read each chapter and answer each question you will feel your heart and your spirit open up. Step by step you will get in touch with the parts of yourself that are sacred and that bring you joy, and when you complete the journey, you will find, as I did, that home really is where your heart is.

Nina Shah

CONTENTS

introduction
26 - 31

ch 2
DISCOVERY
56 - 85

ch 3
DREAMING &
EXPLORING IN COLOR
86 - 109

ch 1
MAKING THE
CONNETION
32 - 55

ch 4
PERMISSION
GRANTED
110 - 131

ch **5**

REAL SPACE
PLANNING
132 - 147

ch **6**

PERSONAL
FURNITURE LAYOUT
148 - 175

ch 7
DIVIDUALIZED
TURE SELECTION
176 - 195

ch 8
BEAUTIFYING
196 - 227

conclusion
228 - 231

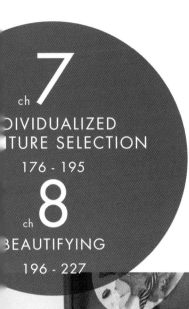

DESIGN ENLIGHTENMENT
COURSE SYLLABUS

STEP 1
DISCOVERY
Exploring your lifestyle

PROCESS
Ask yourself questions that cause introspection of your current lifestyle and help to create your ideal lifestyle *wish list*. This step also reveals your personal and/or family's culture, heritage, and nostalgia.

TOOLS
Discovery Questionnaire

ENLIGHTENMENT
Clarity of purpose and intention. Understanding who you are and your lifestyle.

STEP 2
DREAM
Create a vision board that aligns with your lifestyle and culture

PROCESS
Find images that resonate with experiences you desire to have within your home's spaces.

TOOLS
Mood or Vision Board

ENLIGHTENMENT
Trigger the imagination, tap into your authentic desires for your home.

STEP 3
PERMISSION GRANTED
Evaluate activities and uses for each room in accordance with your lifestyle; *think outside the room*

PROCESS
Use *room bubbles* to group together the functional needs and desires you have selected and place them in appropriate rooms.

TOOLS
Bubble Diagram

ENLIGHTENMENT
Achieve *outside the room* thinking and fit your desires into your rooms.

STEP 4
REAL SPACE PLANNING

Use or create a scaled floor plan in order to gain a better understanding of your actual space

PROCESS
Learn to understand a scaled floor plan as a tool for proper space planning and layout of your furniture.

TOOLS
Floor plans (if available), grid paper, architectural scale and measuring tape.

ENLIGHTENMENT
Understand what really fits in each space as well as traffic flow of each area.

STEP 5
PERSONAL FURNITURE LAYOUT

Assign each space with furniture according to function

PROCESS
Create a furniture layout to support each dream space and desire with alignment.

TOOLS
Scaled floor plan and inspiration photographs from your dream board

ENLIGHTENMENT
Refine and visualize your space as your own.

STEP 6
INDIVIDUALIZED FURNITURE SELECTION

Select furniture to support your personal furniture layout

PROCESS
Make selections of actual furniture pieces that fulfill both the spatial, functional, and spiritual requirements using the descriptives from your questionnaire.

TOOLS
Internet websites, magazines, furniture catalogs

ENLIGHTENMENT
Gain the confidence to know that every furniture selection fits your needs and your spaces.

STEP 7
BEAUTIFY

Accessorize with items that speak to you!

PROCESS
Curate and learn to accessorize like a pro and add details that reflect your unique lifestyle.

TOOLS
Objects from your past, collections, treasured gifts from loved ones and art

ENLIGHTENMENT
Personalize each space with authenic and soulful items that express the real you.

PREFACE

*M*y journey in the creation of this book has been a spiritual one. Now you may say, "How does a book that is centered around a process for interior design tie into one's spiritual journey?" You see, the moment that I started designing, which was usually the minute I had a drawing pencil in my hand or walked into a space, there was only the sheer pleasure of the creative process, which I channeled through my passion for design. I've always instinctively known that being inspired was being in-spirit. And I felt blessed that my journey and my life's mission were one.

Interior design was a full-out joy ride that became second nature to me at a very young age, as natural as breathing. You see I was blessed to have found my passion for creating in this way even before I understood what that meant as a profession. I have clear memories of excitedly rearranging the furniture in my parents' home when I was about ten years old, with the anticipation of Christmas Day joy once my parents came home to see what I had conjured up with our own furniture. By the time I was twelve, I was determined to decorate my own room in antiques. Of course, I didn't even know what an antique was, but I was enamored and literally compulsive about creating a "romantic" look for myself.

I proceeded to save my pennies until the day I could afford my own decorating adventure, since my mother thought my room was just fine the way it was. Finally, the day came that I requested a pilgrimage to numerous thrift shops, which ultimately led to the purchase of a Victorian bedroom set and comforter ensemble from the Spiegel catalog. The set came with a headboard, footboard, nightstand and my favorite item, a dainty sitting vanity, which stayed with me way into adulthood and eventually was handed down to my daughter in later years. I was so proud of what I had created that I even dressed the part for a while, shifting my wardrobe to lacy vintage items culled from a few pieces my grandmother had brought with her from Cuba.

Thus began my obsession with interior design and design in general. I couldn't believe the feelings I was able to summon up in myself once my room had been transformed to my own personal taste and liking. Soon enough, I was studying interior design in the local community college and couldn't wait to start practicing this transformational work for others. By eighteen, my career had officially begun.

me, circa 1981

I quickly discovered I had a talent for sketching and drawing and loved being able to put my ideas on paper with skill. As I began the true practice of design, I worked on commercial projects first and learned all of the technical aspects of bringing a project to reality. These projects included a hospital, hotels, retail stores, and restaurants. I realize now in retrospect that this foundation served to develop the most logical side of my brain and made me an excellent space planner. To this day, I can get lost in the meditative state of working on an empty space and finding the functional layouts within it.

Eventually, I worked my way into residential work and completed my practical education by learning to decorate and accessorize, which are skills that are not necessarily appreciated as much in the commercial world. With this newfound experience of people's homes, I learned to explore the eclectic and very personal aspects of residential design while applying the more practical skills of space planning I learned in the contract realm.

The merger of these two distinct experiences, over the years, allowed me to thrive in my own interior design business and develop a wonderful and steady client following. My success was evident with the continued growth of my business, but something continued to leave me with an empty feeling that I could not fill no matter how many projects I completed or the awards I received. When asked the standard question, "What's your style?" I would literally cringe. I just was not able to reconcile this simple question into a simple answer and ended up annoyed at why it was asked in the first place.

My breakthrough came in December 2014. Just before my birthday, during a three-day business retreat that I had joined to help me as an entrepreneur. Little did I know that out of those three days would come the inspiration for this book and the clarification that my work was not about style at all but instead comes from a much deeper place and a higher purpose. My desires to practice interior design had always stemmed from those early feelings of fulfillment and transformation that I had created for myself when I was just a preteenager. What I really wanted was for everyone to feel the inexplicable satisfaction that a beautifully designed space has the power to create. I knew personally the feelings of joy and elation that could be had when the design of your spaces line up with who you truly are. Capturing this feeling and expressing it as a gift for anyone who would let me was and still is my driving force for creation. Exhilarated by this newfound revelation that it never was about a particular style was liberating, and I set out, just as compulsively as I decorated my first room, to write this book.

This book is designed to reveal to you the awareness and beauty that can be experienced through the proper alignment of your lifestyle with your home. It is my gift to share with my clients and hopefully with you, the process toward *Design Enlightenment.*

It has been a blessing to discover that at this stage in my career I can shift my purpose as a creator to one that can inspire others to fulfill their dreams on a broader scale. I know how powerful it is to feel at home in one's home, and I know the process I have created within these pages will help you enjoy your personal journey of creation and inspire you to live authentic, sacred, and inspired lives.

ACKNOWLEDGMENTS

I would like to express my deepest gratitude to Michelle Villalobos for the tools that helped me ask the deeper questions of *purpose.*

I also want to thank Mina Shah for helping me to organize my thoughts on the page, volunteering to explore the design enlightment process, and offering her loving support.

DEDON - *Garden Hanging* Chair
designed by Fred Frety & Daniel Pouzet
for the Nestrest Collection, 2011

INTRODUCTION

Everyone deserves to have their home feel sacred. Of course this feeling is really more of an attitude that starts from our personal experiences of what sacred means to us. No one can deny the feeling we get when we walk "into" the most sacred space of all, which is not even created by us but exists all around us in nature. When we view a beautiful sunset, or reflections on a lake, the ebb and flow of waves as they hit the sand, these moments are sacred and strike a chord with our subconscious mind that cannot be denied. As we imagine these moments in our lives, we focus on the feelings they bring up in us, and these are the feelings you will have the opportunity to explore in the process of creating *your* sacred spaces.

As in any journey, we start with our first steps. If the destination is distant or untraveled, it helps greatly to have a road map or a guide. I will be offering both. In my many years of creating beautiful and functional interiors as a designer, I have traveled to many personalized destinations for others and can say that as with real traveling, the adventure lies in the uniqueness of the places visited.

It's the unique combination of requirements stemming from the particular individuals' needs and desires that helps to make the journey exciting.

What makes it even more exciting is exploring my clients' unchartered needs, those they haven't even discovered themselves. This inspires me every time. I actually can't begin to create until these needs and desires are clear in my mind, thus becoming my road map. I am always amazed how the landscape of their lives emerges as we begin the exploration process, like an oasis that emerges in the desert, seemingly out of nowhere.

Of course, you might say that I have been trained to create these spaces, and this is true, but the "in-spiration" has not come from training or scholastic skills but rather from my heart. I have seen so many lives transformed by my guidance that I have realized that this ability is actually a gift that needs to be shared. This book is a result of this desire in me. I have been blessed to naturally possess the ability to know how to create these sacred spaces through experience and training.

Now, I have created a process to do that for you. I can tell you with assurance that you will travel uncharted territory, and the destination will truly be a product of your own imagination. You will tap into your heart for the answers to your deepest desires, creating *your* "yellow brick road," taking you safely home. My desire is that this journey will not only be exciting but inspiring and that when we have arrived at our final destination, the sacred spaces we have created together will serve you and your families to live inspired lives. After all, we come home each night to commune or recharge, whether alone or with our families, and as I said before, deserve for these spaces to be our own personal sanctuaries.

"you will
TAP INTO YOUR HEART
for the answers to your deepest desires,
creating your YELLOW BRICK ROAD
taking you safely home"

pause to reflect

CHAPTER 1
MAKING THE CONNECTION

*A*s with any transformative journey, we must start from within. Making the connection to our inner selves and personal yearnings is imperative to becoming aware of ourselves, which ultimately influences our surroundings, as well.

In order to change anything in our lives, our homes, and ultimately in our world, we must make the connection that it is all connected.

Let's begin by the fact that you have been attracted to this book. There is no coincidence in this. You must be in search of the answers found within these pages otherwise it would not be in your hands. I will share my wisdom, gleaned from years of connecting the dots for others. The gifts of design with the gifts of everyone's individuality have provided me with the information that I will generously share, because I believe that happier people create a happier world, and our happiness begins at home.

So if you are asking "what is this book about?" It's easier to explain what it's not about: *Style* just for *style's* sake. Because, *style*, although incredibly important on an emotional level when it comes to creating or igniting inspiration, lacks the ability to create the long-lasting effects and fulfillment that I am seeking to inspire within the pages of this book. I am searching for *something more,* and always felt that beautifully created interior design has the ability to offer a soul stirring experience.

DESIGN
ENLIGHTENMENT
MOMENT

Your style may be as
distinct as your fingerprint
or even more importantly,
a creative reflection of
your soul, and you may
or may not be conscious
of its influence on
you, depending upon
the experiences and
conditioning you may have
had throughout your life
so far.

As we interact with our living spaces we can either be uplifted or not. It is my purpose to help you embark on your personal journey of discovery that reaches beyond the limitations of style. Your style may be as distinct as your fingerprint or even more importantly, a creative reflection of your soul, and you may or may not be conscious of its influence on you, depending upon the experiences and conditioning you may have had throughout your life so far.

Personally, I was blessed to have been born to a mother and father that instinctively, without any formal training, created an environment full of art and beautiful objects that I know led to my path in interior design. I realized later in life, however, that they also were gifted in adding a very special ingredient that was intangible and yet so present in my life. This element was a connection to **spirit**. To this day, I call them my "flower children," and I am incredibly grateful to them for being such a great influence.

So, as we begin to go beyond the ideas of pure style as an influence or the material objects that might reflect our individual tastes, we will take a moment to dive deeper into the meaning behind all of the style decisions we make and hopefully reach a point in which every detail and selection brings us joy. I will venture to bring you a new *awareness* that each design decision makes and brings mindfulness to your interior design. **You will be asked to think about what makes you happy, what objects bring a smile to your face and ultimately what makes you feel good.**

my "flower children"
parents circa 1970s

This book will help you achieve, every day of your life and within your own walls, that experience of walking into a space and feeling lighter and truly at home. Together we will create this experience with a process, and I will give you the tools to do it. We will cultivate a space in your life where you can have all the feelings that you desire and that reflects the deepest part of you. And you get to connect back to spirit.

As I see it, we are all creatures that belong to nature. When we were unable to control our environments, we rose when the sun did and slept when it didn't. We were very "in touch" with our very essence as beings because we had no choice. It was the only way we could survive. Making sure our basic needs were met influenced our lives. *Through nature's influence, we were able to connect to our inner selves and to make decisions based on what we felt inside.* It gave us the opportunity to listen to our inner voice as well as the voice of nature. However, today, we have lost most of our connection to nature. As we control more and more of our environment through modern advances that manipulate our interior world, we have lost all of our connection to nature and thus ourselves. We live in a world that is over stimulating us and we are deeply in need of what nature gave us, which was the ability to relax and be in the present moment and enjoy.

I remember the day that I moved into my new house. This was the first house that my husband and I had ever built from scratch. Every house that we had lived in up until then was an old house. First, a 1926 old Spanish in Coral Gables, then a midcentury modern ranch in South Miami. Even for two people well versed in design and construction (my husband is an Architect and Builder), it was a long process. A year and a half of planning, designing, choosing and building. Finally, it was complete. We enjoyed selecting and implementing new technologies and updates that we had previously only specified for our clients, since all the houses we'd lived in had been older, remodeled homes.

CRICKET
CRICKET

After the year and a half long journey, we were so excited to sleep in our brand new home for the first time, a home which included the use of hurricane-impact-proof windows. In Miami these windows create an extra layer of safety in case of a hurricane. We were excited to be so well protected from the elements and saw this as a pure benefit. A benefit they were, but they did something else that was totally unexpected. They blocked out all the sounds. Sounds from the street. Sounds from outside. And because of this, it turned out I couldn't sleep! Not from excitement of a new room to enjoy but from the deafening silence these windows created.

All of the houses we had before had old windows that allowed for noise to filter in and I didn't realize how much the sounds from the outside had been a comforting influence for me. I became restless without the noises that lulled me to sleep. All of those years, somehow, those noises had become part of my connection to self-relaxation and acted like lullabies. **This contrast made me aware of how much the sounds of nature relaxed me, and it led me to make a connection in myself about how sounds could influence our experience in an environment.**

I'm not saying that we have to give up all of our contemporary comforts, but I am saying that at our very core we are creatures of nature that have to learn to reconnect with our natural selves, our inner rhythms and our awareness of the interior spaces we live in. This plays such a big role in how we feel. I know that design, especially conscious design, can help do this because I have watched my client's lives transform and feelings shift because of simple adjustments within these spaces I've created. I'm here to help bring clarity to this disconnect in our inner lives and our inner spaces and tie the two together for you so that you can feel truly joyful in your home, because at our very core we are a part of nature, and we respond to it whether we understand it or not, whether we feel it or not, whether we recognize it or not.

If you're camping out in the wilderness with a tent, you cannot help but be in touch with nature. It's an amazing experience because it influences you from the core. From the inside out—you're connected.

So how do we get connected to that again? How do we recognize that connection without living in a tree? It is my belief that we have created a tear in the fabric of our lives that needs mending. We rarely eat together, in our own homes. We rarely talk to each other, we might text each other instead. We're looking at a screen for distraction and for relaxation instead of having a conversation or reading, and a simple change of furniture placement can make all that change.

This relates to design because as we've evolved in the way we interact within our walls, the way we design our interiors to support our lives has lagged behind in the past. We're so heavily influenced by outside stimuli controlled by man, not nature, that we're becoming a society disconnecting even further and further from our basic needs for communion.

A large part of this has to do with the evolution of design as it has influenced our interior spaces. ***Design*** is **the "selection and organization of materials and forms to fulfill a particular function,"** as stated in one of my earliest interior design textbooks by Ray and Sarah Faulkner, Inside Today's Home. They also say:

> Design as we understand it today is an intrinsically *conscious* process, the deliberate act of forming materials to fit a certain function, whether utilitarian or aesthetic. Still, the marvelous structures built by animals do refer to one of our most fundamental ideas of design- the so-called "grand design" of nature. From the tiniest unique snowflake to the mightiest mountain range, we find our world beautiful, satisfying, appropriate in short well-designed.

"at our very core
WE ARE CREATURES OF NATURE
that have to learn to reconnect with our natural selves,
our inner rhythms and our awareness of the interior
spaces we live in"

These statements could not be more true when it comes to the essence of design and how we are influenced by these ideas in our homes.

Have you ever wondered why our homes are designed the way they are? Well, I'll give you a little snapshot of what has happened to get us to where we are today. As we began seeking shelter indoors, our initial dwellings were primitive but very in touch with nature. However, as we evolved to create the civilizations that we currently have, our sophistication led to several distinct developments in the way we design our homes.

Mediterranean Courtyard

Our architecture has pretty much always been an artistic expression of our basic needs. The needs to have access to water and cook with fire were the most basic influencers for the designs of our homes in the early stages of development. In fact, what is known today as the *Mediterranean Floor Plan*, **which were rooms surrounding an interior courtyard exposed to the elements,** began in Greek and Roman times when light and water were intrinsic in the center of the home's design for daily and easy access.

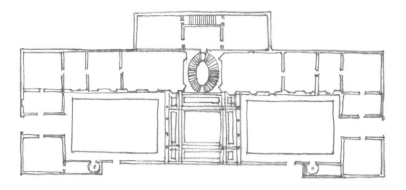

Later on, as our priorities changed, protection and security took precedent, and the fortress-like castle became a reflection of that requirement. These spaces were tended to by many servants or helpers in order to bring the necessities of food and water in to make them functional environments. This concept of the classical floor plan continued to evolve, but the basic rooms of the house required the constant tending of by others, thus creating an atmosphere of formality.

Oddly enough, even though most of us don't live in castles, that concept of formality is still reflected in the layout of our homes today. The challenge, however, is that the average home does not have the convenience of multiple servants to tend to our every need. **These separate and boxed-in rooms, one after the other, separated by walls and distinct divisions,** became the *classical floor plan* most commonly used in our designs up until the *modern era,* **which introduced the idea of opening up the spaces to each other.**

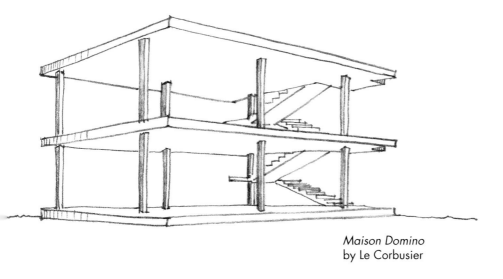

Maison Domino
by Le Corbusier

One of the major influencers of our time and therefore the way we design our spaces was the prominent American architect, Frank Lloyd Wright, who began to challenge and explore how we live and brought a more organic and therefore modern approach to architecture. His interpretation of how an American home should be designed, greatly impacted our design history. For Wright, the Hearth or fireplace was at the core of family life, very similar to essential fire for primitive cave dwellers.

However, just as Wright's priority was the gathering of family around a warm fire, our new hearth has become the Television. We have most certainly become screen obsessed. This device as well as our computers and phones have transformed our lives and have made old-fashioned rooms like living rooms and dining rooms an abandoned leftover from the classical past.

Why are these history lessons important to cover? Because they are subliminally influencing our interiors to this day. We are still designing our homes without asking ourselves if our homes still serve and support us. We may have some abandoned rooms leftover from our past that are not being used.

I'm here to bring to the forefront of our minds that our homes have, by default, become a bit of the past with a bit of the present and have not quite evolved in a way that makes sense for our lives today.

I hope to bring new awareness to these incongruencies so that we can adjust our homes to suit our lifestyles.

We can't begin to create this alignment with our spaces and make them sacred to us without the knowledge of its history or the awareness of why it exists in our lives in the first place.

As a designer, I have created so many beautiful spaces, but the ones I am the most proud of are the ones that build memories for the people that live there. My philosophy for design is and has always been about those individuals that will ultimately live in the space, and I relish in the highest expression of that.

With a new awareness of the historic influences we are still experiencing in our interiors, along with our own personal family conditioning, we can give ourselves permission to use our rooms as we see fit.

The good news is that with a new awareness of ourselves, of our habits, and a few simple steps, we can help to get ourselves back in balance by adjusting our interior spaces to instill more communion with ourselves, our families, and our purpose.

You may be asking, "Can design really do this?" Absolutely! I'll give you an example! I've just finished remodeling the shoe store of one of my dearest friends. The original design was pretty typical of a retail boutique store design. It had two separate seating banquets that by their design and placement required people to face outward and not see each other while trying on shoes. Since I frequented this charming boutique often, I was very familiar with the relaxed ambiance and culture of the store ,and I felt it would benefit from a different concept that was more interactive and akin to a lounge environment versus its rigid furniture placement. I opted to replace the ottomans for two loveseats facing each other with a large ottoman in between them and lots of other smaller tables and poofs to pull and gather around the larger pieces. Simple, right? After the furniture change, the transformation was magical.

With a new awareness of the historic influences we are still experiencing in our interiors along with our own personal family conditioning we can give ourselves permission to use our rooms as we see fit. We can help to get ourselves back in balance by adjusting our interior spaces to instill more communion with ourselves, our families, and our purpose.

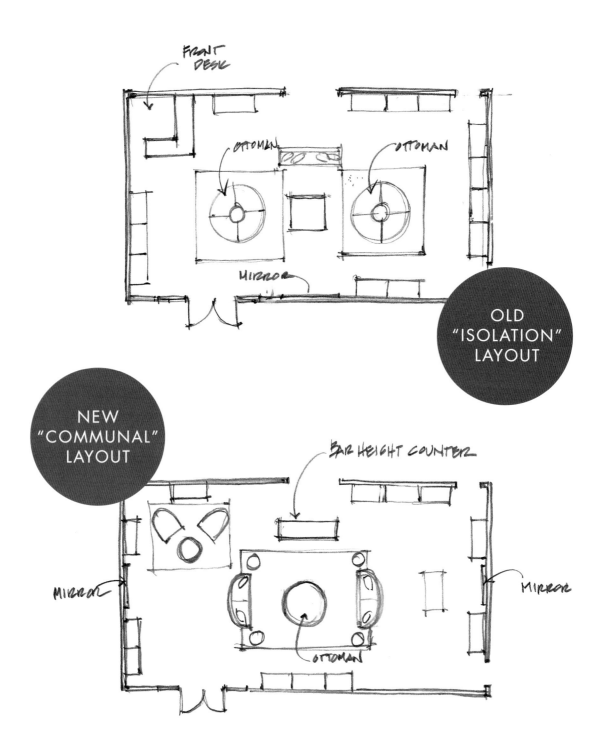

FRONT DESK

OTTOMAN

OTTOMAN

MIRROR

OLD "ISOLATION" LAYOUT

NEW "COMMUNAL" LAYOUT

BAR HEIGHT COUNTER

MIRROR

MIRROR

OTTOMAN

I watched how people's behavior completely transformed. They began to interact in the space in a completely different way. People were hanging out, talking to each other and overall enjoying the time spent selecting their shoes. They even felt free enough to sit on the floor rug. Most importantly, no one wanted to rush out the door, and the more time they spent in the space, the more they made new friends, with the added benefit to the shop owner of buying more shoes. Suddenly, somebody sitting on the loveseat trying on a pair was next to another lady saying, "Wow, those are so nice," and then going to the mirror and coming back, saying, "I really like those! I want to try those on, too." The entire buying experience became a whole new interaction. As I watched it, I became fascinated by the way people behaved before and after the change of furniture and layout.

*The point I'm making here is that by changing the way people sat through furniture placement, I was able to change the way they **felt** in the space. By creating a more relaxed environment that felt more at home, I was able to establish a sense of community. The behavior changed by simply changing the furniture, and the vibe that was created was truly enchanting to watch. Instead of just buying shoes, they were **interacting** with each other while buying shoes. The space became a communal living room rather than just a store.*

This magical transformation in people's behavior is what was so interesting to me as a designer, especially because it happened in a public space. It made me believe that we can and *should* do this at home as well. That great feeling that we can experience in hotels, coffee shops and even office work spaces has begun to open our eyes to a new experience of what a vibrant interior space looks and feels like. Why not consciously bring these ideas home to invigorate those neglected or unused spaces, like the unlived-in living room and the undined-in dining room?

This experience inspired me to give a wonderful talk at the FIU Interior Architectural Symposium, *Blurred Lines*, where these concepts were the topic of discussion, specifically how this shift in attitude is already happening in public spaces. I recently observed an example of this when a friend of mine moved into a brand-new building in Fort Lauderdale, and the lobby has a communal bar and a kitchen, two lounges, and a library-like lounge. The whole place has a "Let's get together! It's our own living room … our own space!" kind of feeling that made me smile. There was an eclectic mix of furnishings that invited relaxation and use, emphasis on the word "use." When would you have seen a lobby like that in the past?

Before, you would walk into these lobbies, and it was as if the sofas were telling you, "You're not supposed to sit here. I'm just here to be pretty." I really don't think this kind of feeling serves us as a society, and I think we are all getting that! This "don't touch," "don't sit" kind of living just doesn't work and quite frankly should be eliminated from our mentality.

I don't believe we want to live in spaces that are just sucking air and empty! I call them the *abandoned rooms*. We've conditioned ourselves to the point of disconnection, and it's time for a change. It's time for an evolution, one in which we are connected—to our homes, to our families, and to our spirit.

So, now I'm sure you're asking, "How do I do this? How do I bring this sense of purpose and spirit into my home?"

That is what this book is for. It's designed to help you take this journey with me in the recreation of your home's interior spaces. We will take it one step at a time, because as I often say at my design studio, **creating an interior is like eating a whale; you can only take one bite at a time.** We will start with the very first *bite*, which is asking yourself questions that will begin to create awareness of things you probably had never thought of before, especially in terms of your home and your connection to it.

Each baby step or "small bite" will take you closer and closer to the ultimate goal of what I like to call "Design Enlightenment." I promise I'm here to hold your hand throughout the steps and make it easy for you. I'll even give you video tutorials at the stages in which visuals are more effective than words on a page.

I hope by now you are excited and ready to move your furniture and change your life! I will give you some of my favorite furniture layouts to play with at home as well as the right questions to ask yourself in order to become aware of design *intention.*

Let's get ready to design, not just for shelter or survival but to add spirit, intention, and purpose to our spaces and allow them to be expressions of our beautiful and blessed lives and ourselves. When you come from this place of awareness, you will literally experience a transformation in your life and the lives of the loved ones that have the pleasure of spending time in your home. Let's begin!

REVIEW OF TERMS

AWARENESS

Knowledge or perception of a situation or fact. Well-informed interest.

DESIGN

The selection and organization of materials and forms to fulfill a particular function.

MEDITERRANEAN FLOORPLAN

An architectural design in which rooms surround an interior courtyard exposed to the elements, which began in Greek and Roman times when light and water were intrinsic to the function of daily life.

CLASSICAL FLOORPLAN

An architectural layout and design usually derived from the principles of Greek and Roman architecture of antiquity in which rooms were laid out side by side.

MODERN ERA

This term is applied to modernist movements at the turn of the 20th Century and schools of design that were reconciling the principles of architectural design with the technological advances of the time in reaction to classical ideas that preceded it.

INTENTION

The mental state that represents a commitment to carrying out an action in the future; planning for a result with significant thought.

CHAPTER RECAP

Making the Connection

The Foundation for Design Enlightenment is Awareness

In this chapter, you've started to realize that changing the way we place our furniture in a room can either gather us together or send us apart. We have become more aware of the connection between ourselves and our interiors, as well as our behaviors within them.

"Knowing others is wisdom, knowing yourself is enlightenment."

—Lao Tsu

pause to reflect

CHAPTER 2
STEP 1—DISCOVERY

Tools

Personal Imprint Questionnaire

Enlightenment

Clarity of Purpose and Intention / Sensory Tips

To start our discovery process, we need to dive deeply into our "interior," and ironically it's not at all about our interior spaces; it's truly about our inside space, the one that lies in our minds and creates the world around us. I think the very word "interior" is metaphorical for me and should be for you, because we can't explore what we want to surround ourselves with until we explore and reflect on what we are inside.

I always thought my calling was in the creation of beauty in the outside world as reflected by my work as an interior designer. I feel this is a gift, and I have enjoyed sharing it with so many of my wonderful clients throughout the thirty years of creating for them. Today, however, my philosophy has expanded to a much greater purpose, and I want to share how to begin the exploration of your interior in order to help you bring your best *interiors* to life. I will be your personal guide in this process. We will make wonderful discoveries together and hopefully have great "aha moments" to inspire our work together.

So, how do we do this, you ask? Well *asking* is exactly the first step. We ask questions that will conjure up memories of what brings us joy, and comfort, and happiness and translate those answers into our interiors. These simple discoveries lead to powerful shifts in our thinking, which, in turn, transform our day-to-day lives and lifestyles.

Let's take a moment to think of the homes we grew up in.

What did they look like?

What kind of furniture did they have?

How did you feel in the rooms that your parents created for you?

As I ask these simple questions, you can already recall whether your family was a "sit down around a well-set table" type of family or maybe an "open up the TV table" type of family. How we felt in the homes of our early childhood and the rituals that we experienced surrounding these rooms we lived in created an imprint that influence our decisions and desires today. If we had positive experiences in our dining rooms, we are much more likely to want to make this room a special place in our homes.

In my home, dining was important and a daily ritual, but it was on the casual side, and I never recall having a very formal dinner, except for Thanksgiving, which is pretty typical of most, and even this was buffet style, because we are a big Cuban family. Therefore, dining for me was very important, though, without a lot of pretense, but sacred as well because it was a daily ritual for catching up with each other as a family and winding down before bedtime. Everyone has these little snippets of memories. You really can't think of your entire childhood, but you do have these little moments. And these can be positive or negative and have **conditioned** your ideas about your interiors and how you use them.

Take a moment to bring these memories back and make of note of them if you'd like in the "pause to reflect" page at the end of this chapter. They will be useful to you as you continue on this journey.

What were the activities that you remember most fondly?

Were they around the dinner table?

Were they around the bedroom getting tucked in?

Were they around sitting on your grandma's lap in that comfy chair?

How we felt in the house of our early childhood and the rituals that we experienced surrounding these rooms we lived in created an imprint that influence our decisions and desires today.

When it came time to raise my children, I created a very similar ritual around my dining room. I literally used my dining table every day in a very casual and approachable way, and this ritual has grown to include our grandchildren. I noticed that the hectic life that my daughter lived didn't allow her to make dining all together as a family into a daily ritual, so I came up with "Tuesday night dinners," because I wanted my grandkids to experience what it was like to sit around a table surrounded by family.

Those memories of laughing and sharing the mishaps and adventures of the day with each other were deeply imbedded in my memory. My childhood memories around dining were and still are so precious to me that I could not imagine my kids, or my grandkids, not having this seemingly simple ritual in their lives. This ritual still exists in my life today even though the Tuesday night thing is not necessarily Tuesday only.

Now, of course, not all memories are so fondly recalled. I remember asking a client during the discovery process this one question, "So how did your family have dinner?" and I got a very different answer from what I experienced and what my grandchildren are experiencing.

In fact, it was quite the opposite. Dining for this client was not dining at all but more like eating at any improvised location, because she grew up as the daughter of a single parent, her father. He worked most of the day and was only able to bring her food, usually of the "fast" variety, during the day, and then he ran out to continue working. That was pretty much it, until one day, a "mother" appeared in her life as a new and domineering figure that had come to bring order out of such chaos, or so she thought. In doing so and in her eagerness to instill some semblance of domesticity into her new family's life, she swung the pendulum in the opposite direction. So rigid were her rituals in getting ready for dinner that it became a military-style affair, complete with the perfectionism of her dominating style, thus creating an atmosphere of fear and dread for her children. If the table wasn't set just right, there was hell to pay. Needless to say, the emotions attached to "dining" for my client were firmly wrapped around these two extremes. Total improvised informality or perfection and rigidness, neither one being much fun at all. These emotions became a blockage for the whole dining room thing for her—so much so that any memory of eating at a table was tainted. When I asked this simple and seemingly innocent question about her brand-new adult version of a dining room, I was met with such resistance that it became a "design therapy" session. Luckily, we broke through this barrier, and today she embraces her newfound joy in the dining room, her way, her style, with just the right blend of structure and without formality at all. Which, I have to say, is the point of this story.

It's about finding out what is right for you in regards to these spaces we give labels to, without the preconceived notions of someone else's life.

This is totally about what works for you, and I grant you the FREEDOM and permission to use your rooms, *all of them*, as you wish. There you go. The teacher has announced recess, and you can come out and PLAY, IN ALL OF YOUR ROOMS.

So, what were your feelings wrapped around dinner or lunch or being at home having a meal? See how this simple question about how you ate can conjure up so many emotions? Most of us have all of these nostalgic *imprints* of our homes and the activities we share in them.

We also have distinct habitual behaviors that create our preferences for the creation of our sacred spaces. These preferences have to do with our own way of doing certain activities well and feeling successful and happy doing them, such as reading and studying or cooking or crafting. We all know how we feel most comfortable doing any of these things. Often noise or lack of it is a huge influence in our choices.

For example, when designing home offices for my clients, I have discovered that there is not one standard furniture layout that fits all. This is because everyone has their own personal preference for this activity or task based on their individual working style. Some people prefer to be out in the open and want to have their desks facing out toward the room or at least a window. Others prefer to be in a cloistered or enclosed space in order to better focus and avoid distraction from outside sources.

I remember a specific request by a client, to create a desk with all of the typical necessities, in his closet. At first I thought it quite odd, but later I realized it made perfect sense; by having his desk in the closet, he could have his quiet time without the interruptions from spouse or children that prevented him from being able to complete a task.

In complete contrast, I've created desks for children to do their homework in their bedrooms only to discover from parent feedback that their children prefer to be at a communal table like the breakfast room, gathered around family in order to feel connected with others as they complete their projects. In other words, this is personal. **Ask yourself the right questions, and you'll create the best sacred spaces for you. Recognize your own behavioral preferences, and you'll be even more attuned to your own needs as you create.**

*This is exactly what the discovery process is about: looking at the interior—of **yourself**, that is—and discovering what you enjoy, what you don't, what you had, and what you wished you had.*

By doing this, you can create something that honors the past or not, by creating what is sacred to you and allows for complete and unlimited possibility, allowing you to explore what inspires you.

SO LET'S DISCOVER!

In these next pages, you will answer questions that will allow you to discover your preferences and become aware of the memories and conditions that have made up your *personal design imprint.*

This questionnaire is the tool for laying the foundation of the playtime that will come later on our journey to *enlightened design.* Because discovery is what it's all about, if you're not asked the right questions at this stage, or if you're not honest in your answers, it's impossible to dive into the next steps. So make sure to be honest with your answers and take time to explore the feelings each question brings up.

Before we dive into any of the typical tasks of decorating a home, like picking out furniture and colors, there are a few things we need to know in order to make this process fun, seamless, and enjoyable!

The following questionnaire will help you gain the awareness that you need in order to select and design your rooms with an enlightened approach that will be in alignment with who *you* are.

DISCOVERY QUESTIONNAIRE

SECTION A: Discovery—Becoming Aware

1. When you were a child, what activities or pastimes do you remember most fondly at home?
Select at least three from this helpful list or add your own.

☐ PLAYING INSIDE   ☐ DANCING

☐ PLAYING OUTSIDE   ☐ EXERCISING

☐ GARDENING   ☐ RELAXING

☐ READING   ☐ SOCIALIZING

☐ SINGING   ☐ EATING

☐ CRAFTING   ☐ BATHING

☐ STUDYING   ☐ DRAWING/PAINTING

☐ CONVERSING   ☐ COOKING

☐ PLAYING MUSIC   ☐ ENTERTAINING

☐ LISTENING TO MUSIC   ☐ BUILDING

☐ WATCHING TV/MOVIES   ☐ NAPPING/SLEEPING

☐ ROLE PLAYING/ACTING   ☐ OTHER: _____

☐ WORKING

2. When you look at the activities you picked from question 1, what emotions do you recall feeling from these activities?

3.   As an adult, what activities or pastimes do you engage in most often at home?
Here is another helpful list.

☐ PLAYING	☐ DANCING
☐ MEDITATING	☐ EXERCISING
☐ GARDENING	☐ RELAXING
☐ READING	☐ SOCIALIZING
☐ SINGING	☐ EATING
☐ CRAFTING	☐ BATHING
☐ STUDYING	☐ DRAWING/PAINTING
☐ CONVERSING	☐ COOKING
☐ PLAYING MUSIC	☐ ENTERTAINING
☐ LISTENING TO MUSIC	☐ BUILDING
☐ WATCHING TV/MOVIES	☐ NAPPING/SLEEPING
☐ ROLE PLAYING/ACTING	☐ OTHER: _____
☐ WORKING	

4.   List these activities in order of importance and state whether your home supports these activities well.

1) _____   ☐YES   ☐NO   ☐NOT SURE

2) _____   ☐YES   ☐NO   ☐NOT SURE

3) _____   ☐YES   ☐NO   ☐NOT SURE

4) _____   ☐YES   ☐NO   ☐NOT SURE

5) _____   ☐YES   ☐NO   ☐NOT SURE

5.   Let's look at the list again and select activities that you **would like** to include in your lifestyle at home that are currently missing.

☐ PLAYING   ☐ DANCING

☐ MEDITATING   ☐ EXERCISING

☐ GARDENING   ☐ RELAXING

☐ READING   ☐ SOCIALIZING

☐ SINGING   ☐ EATING

☐ CRAFTING   ☐ BATHING

☐ STUDYING   ☐ DRAWING/PAINTING

☐ CONVERSING   ☐ COOKING

☐ PLAYING MUSIC   ☐ ENTERTAINING

☐ LISTENING TO MUSIC   ☐ BUILDING

☐ WATCHING TV/MOVIES   ☐ NAPPING/SLEEPING

☐ ROLE PLAYING/ACTING   ☐ OTHER: _____

☐ WORKING

6.   Do you see a connection or disconnection between what you enjoyed as a child versus as an adult? If so, why do you believe this is?

7.   What areas in your home do you spend the most time in?

☐ LIVING ROOM   ☐ FAMILY ROOM

☐ DINING ROOM   ☐ KITCHEN

☐ BREAKFAST ROOM   ☐ TERRACE

☐ PORCH   ☐ STUDY

☐ LIBRARY   ☐ DEN

☐ OFFICE   ☐ EXERCISE ROOM

☐ BEDROOM   ☐ BATHROOM

☐ RECREATIONAL ROOM   ☐ OTHER: _____

8.   Elaborate on what activities you do most in these rooms, even if these rooms are not intended for that use.

SECTION B: Dream—Use Your Imagination

Now you have an opportunity to create what you want. A lifestyle that reflects your values, your preferences, and who you are. **It's time to *dream*!**

When you have dreams about your ideal living situation, how do you see it? Are you having big family dinners? Do you have a quiet reading area? Where is the energy in the hous e the greatest? What is your kitchen like? Do you enjoy outdoor living? What is your bedroom like? Write in as many details as you can, describing your ideal home and lifestyle. Remember, the sky's the limit. Express what you would love to have, and we can always tailor from there. Remember to explore how you feel in each room and let that be your guide.

This activity can be explored with others like friends or family. Not only is it fun to share, but it also might help to get your imagination going.

1.   I have always wanted to have a space for...

2.   My ideal home has...

3.   Is there anything you have always wanted but dismissed because it does not seem possible or practical? Write it here!
Something I have always thought would be fun would be...

4.   Is there any area in your home where you would like to spend more time but don't right now due to spatial constraints, design, layout, or something else? List them here.

5.   While dreaming about your ideal home and lifestyle, which spaces and activities bring you the most joy?

SECTION C: Define

Use the following list to help refine and define your personal preferences for the feelings, materials, textures, and style of your home. Feel free to choose as many as you wish.

1. How would you like your home to *feel?*

☐ COMFORTABLE ☐ CALMING/SOOTHING

☐ RELAXED ☐ EXCITING

☐ FUN ☐ HAPPY

☐ INVIGORATING ☐ STIMULATING

☐ PEACEFUL ☐ THOUGHTFUL

☐ REFRESHING ☐ INVITING

☐ FRESH ☐ LUXURIOUS

☐ STRONG ☐ BOLD

☐ REFINED ☐ VIBRANT

☐ LOUD ☐ QUIET

☐ BRIGHT ☐ AIRY

☐ CLEAN ☐ SERENE

☐ OTHER: _____ ☐ OTHER: _____

thoughtful

family photos
favorite books
travel mementos

graphic prints
contrasting colors
oversized elements

bold

relaxed

soft throws
comby pillows
natural elements

luxurious

polished stone
shiny metal
glass & crystal

2.   What are the *materials* and *textures* you want to experience in your home?

MATERIALS	TEXTURES
☐ WOOD	☐ SOFT
☐ FABRIC	☐ FLUFFY
☐ METAL	☐ SHINY
☐ LEATHER	☐ SMOOTH
☐ BRICK	☐ EARTHY
☐ STONE	☐ SLEEK
☐ CONCRETE	☐ DISTRESSED/RUSTIC
☐ GLASS	☐ MATTE
☐ ACRYLIC/LUCITE	☐ NATURAL/ORGANIC
☐ FELT	☐ WOVEN
☐ MIRROR	☐ SATIN
☐ OTHER: _____	☐ OTHER: _____

my daugter's dream catcher showcasing a variety of textures from shiny and smooth acrylic, soft and supple suede, shimmering feathers over a fluffy rug

3.   What words would you use to describe your ideal home *style*?

☐ ANTIQUE   ☐ URBAN

☐ MINIMAL   ☐ SHABBY CHIC

☐ TRADITIONAL   ☐ ECLECTIC

☐ CLASSIC/TIMELESS   ☐ BOHEMIAN

☐ CONSERVATIVE   ☐ RETRO

☐ FLASHY   ☐ ARTISTIC

☐ COUNTRY   ☐ GLAMOROUS

☐ FRENCH   ☐ COLORFUL

☐ MEDITERRANEAN   ☐ ASIAN

☐ VINTAGE   ☐ COSMOPOLITAN

☐ CONTEMPORARY   ☐ ENGLISH

☐ ANGULAR   ☐ AMERICANA

☐ MODERN   ☐ COASTAL

☐ OTHER: _____   ☐ OTHER: _____

Coastal &
Contemporary

Classic &
Minimal

Traditional &
Glamorous

Asian/
Ethnic

SECTION D: Finishing Touches

The following section adds the personal and finishing touches to complete your spaces.

1.   What accessories do you own that are meaningful to you and that you would like displayed in your home?

2.   Do you have anything that's been packed away for a while that you would use in your home? Why?

3.   Is there a special collection you have or would like to have displayed in your home? Elaborate on how you see this. Does it need any special room, furniture, or accessory?

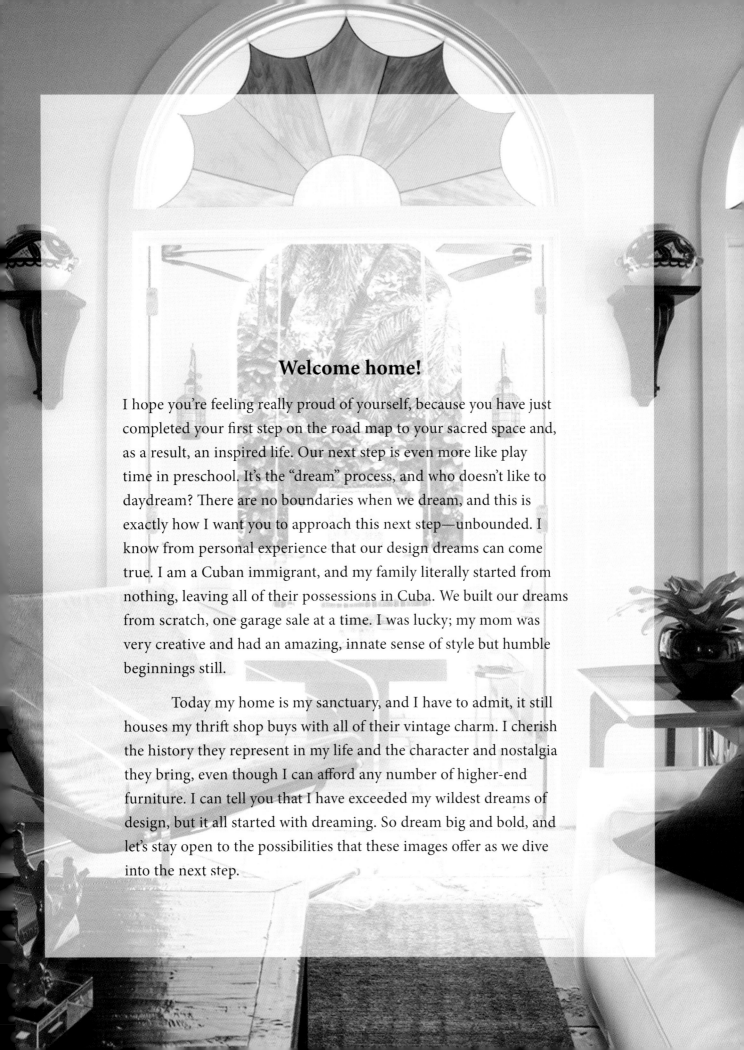

Welcome home!

I hope you're feeling really proud of yourself, because you have just completed your first step on the road map to your sacred space and, as a result, an inspired life. Our next step is even more like play time in preschool. It's the "dream" process, and who doesn't like to daydream? There are no boundaries when we dream, and this is exactly how I want you to approach this next step—unbounded. I know from personal experience that our design dreams can come true. I am a Cuban immigrant, and my family literally started from nothing, leaving all of their possessions in Cuba. We built our dreams from scratch, one garage sale at a time. I was lucky; my mom was very creative and had an amazing, innate sense of style but humble beginnings still.

Today my home is my sanctuary, and I have to admit, it still houses my thrift shop buys with all of their vintage charm. I cherish the history they represent in my life and the character and nostalgia they bring, even though I can afford any number of higher-end furniture. I can tell you that I have exceeded my wildest dreams of design, but it all started with dreaming. So dream big and bold, and let's stay open to the possibilities that these images offer as we dive into the next step.

REVIEW OF TERMS

IMPRINT

To cause something to stay in your mind or memory; make a mark.

DREAM

Contemplate the possibility of doing something; an idea or vision that is created in your imagination; something that you have wanted very much to be or have for long time.

CONDITIONED

A response that has been learned and accustomed from our past that may or not serve our present lifestyle.

Discovery

Sifting and Sorting through Personal Preferences

How do you feel? And what have you discovered about yourself? My hope is that you have begun a dialogue of curiosity that will fuel you to the next step in the process. In this chapter, you answered questions that helped you discern your feelings and your sensory and style preferences. These answers will guide you along your discovery path and serve to influence all of your future choices as part of your design enlightenment.

"My mission in life is not merely to survive but to thrive; and to do so with some passion, some humor, and some style."

— Maya Angelou

pause to reflect

"our
FEELINGS
inspire the
thoughts that
CREATE
THE WORLD
AROUND US"

CHAPTER 3
STEP 2: DREAMING
AND EXPLORING COLOR

Tools

Dream Board

Enlightenment

Tap into Your Authentic Desires and Trigger the Imagination

I am a firm believer that our feelings inspire the thoughts that create the world around us. As a creator of interiors and furniture, I am always in a state of wonderment by this process, because for me it always begins with an image or dream in my head. It is truly second nature to me and the reason why I love using pin-up boards in my design studio. This visual tool allows us to brainstorm and gather inspiration for my projects. So we begin the next step in your journey in much the same way as I begin my projects, with a simple pin-up tool that helps to inspire the dreaming process. By now you've made a connection with your desires—you've started to think about your home in more than just a "Let's throw some furniture in this room" way and are asking, "Why am I placing *this* furniture in *that* room?"

You've explored some of your innermost desires through your Dicsovery Questionnaire and are ready to dream and dream big, this time with images rather than words. This step is wonderful! I always ask my clients to gather images and pictures of what they want in their home, and today this process is so much simpler than before. We have a plethora of images at our fingertips and can literally search through thousands of images with one click. Of course, we can also sit with great magazines as well. When I was a kid, my mom played this game with us when we were bored, especially on a road trip. She would say, "Now look for anything red," and we would start searching for red objects surrounding us. Suddenly our attention would turn to the suggestion of the color red, and it would miraculously come into focus. It always amazed me that until the suggestion was made we wouldn't make this observation. So now I will play my mom's role in this next part of the game of creating your sacred space.

As you search for the images to create your dream board, observe the *feelings* that the images evoke. By this I mean that you do not need to go straight to design or decorating magazines in order to begin gathering your images. Be a bit more ***abstract*** or general.

You may look at a travel magazine and stop longingly at an image of a Tuscan Villa. The colors of the walls, the warmth, the idea of eating delicious food in an outdoor setting. Or maybe a tropical beach setting where the colors of the ocean become your inspiration for the room you've dreamed of having.

Focus on your feelings first, as these are the indicators of your heart's desires.

A sacred space begins when your heartstrings are pulled in a new direction; one that *feels* like home. If a sparkling cityscape attracts you, then go with that. Save the image and put it on your dream board. It might be the glittery lights and urban setting that truly make you happy.

*Whatever attracts you—and most importantly why it attracts you—is what you should go with. Ask **why** when you look at the picture, and you will promptly have an answer unique to you. Only you know the **why**. It is your personal inspiration. How great is that?*

As you group your images you will start to create what I call a **dream board**.

The dream board allows you to explore things that you really love—not on a conscious level, but more on a subconscious level. This is the level where true manifestation occurs.

Images do that for us. So when clients come to me, and they have done their homework by gathering pictures either pulled out of magazines or collected on Houzz or Pinterest, I ask them questions using *their* pictures. I ask them, "What do you like about this picture?" Or even more importantly, "How does this picture make you feel?"

This is a very important part of the process. So here you will ask yourself the important questions. For example, "What do I like about this picture and why?" It will help you understand your own desires and why you are drawn to certain things. I had a client that shared a picture with me that she said she loved. When I asked her the question, "What do you like about this picture?" what I discovered was that her attraction to this picture, which was a beautiful neutral and elegantly casual room, was not at all what had possessed her to tear the picture out. In fact, the only reason she had selected this picture was because of the flowers on the table in the room. The only thing she loved about it was the flowers. That blew me away! I couldn't believe that the flowers, which happened to be a gorgeous shade of fuchsia, were the focus of her inspiration. Her answer was, "Oh my God, yes, I love those flowers. Look at the color!" And I said, "Oh, so you really like that *color*?" She said, "Yes, I love that color. I'd love to see that color somewhere." At that moment, I understood that she wasn't afraid of bold colors, and to her, this color meant living boldly and with happiness. Needless to say, I went on to translate her color attraction into fabrics and accessories that really resonated with her, personally.

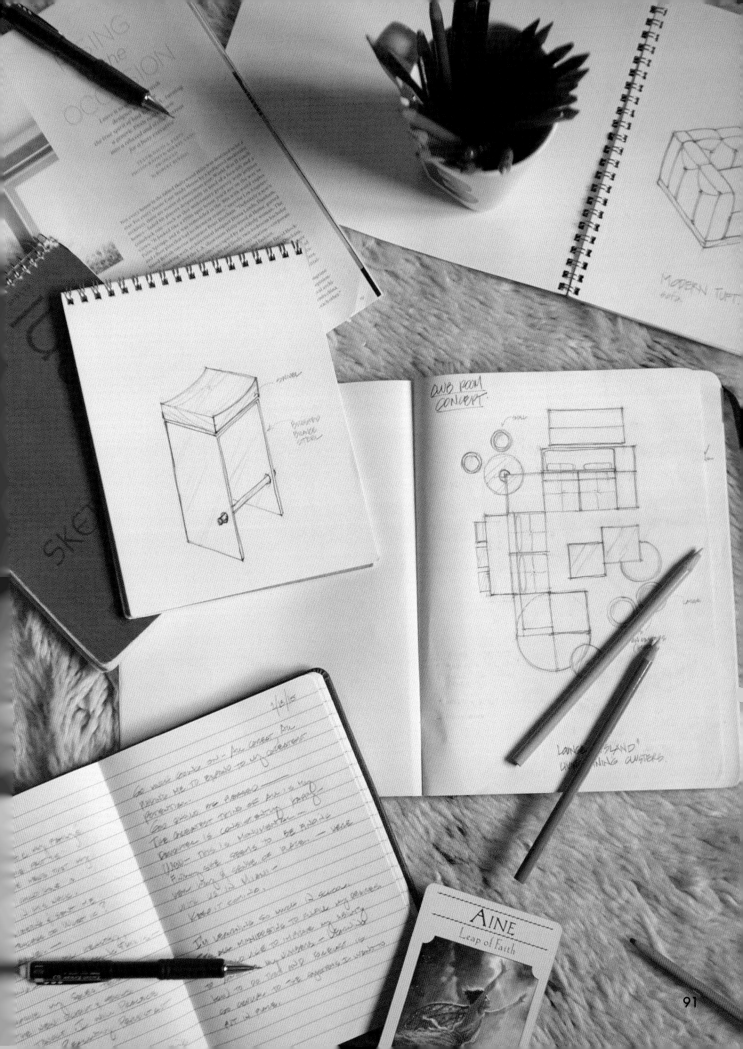

DESIGN
ENLIGHTENMENT
MOMENT

Knowing **what** you want will allow you to furnish your home mindfully. Knowing **why** you want it is design enlightenment! It's understanding yourself and honoring yourself so that the interiors of your home are a reflection of *you*!

The awakening for me was that before asking *that* question, I was coming to all kinds of different conclusions that came from my experiences and not hers. "Well, maybe it's the sofa. Maybe it's the shape of the chair. Maybe it's the rug." No! It was the flowers. I am always amazed and often surprised by the answers I get during this interview session using images. Very often, the reasons given are not at all the ones I thought they would be, and this is why we need to continue to ask ourselves these questions as we create our dream boards.

As you create your own dream board, you will have the opportunity to explore your color preferences with a new understanding of the basics of color principles and why they make us feel the way they do, which I will explain further along in this chapter.

Knowing *what* you want will allow you to furnish your home mindfully. Knowing *why* you want it is design enlightenment! It's understanding yourself and honoring yourself so that the interiors of your home are a reflection of *you*!

We all have an idea of what we think we want. But then you get it, and for some reason you're not as excited as you thought you would be. "I thought it's what I wanted … but" … and that's because we *thought* about it and didn't *feel* it.

There's nothing worse than that disconnect, and it's what I have found can make interior design stressful for some. As you create your dream board, you will make discoveries about yourself that will help you avoid the stress of misalignment with yourself or with your designer, should you decide to use a professional in this process.

You are going to create a visual representation of what you truly desire. It's important that you do this step visually and physically and not just in your head.

Some people do it through magazines. I personally like the physical touch of a magazine. Some people do it through digital methods, gathering images online. What's fun is that you get to collect pictures just for the sake of self-exploration. You're not really tied to anything; you haven't bought it yet. You're just *dreaming*.

Step one to creating a dream board is to let your mind be expansive. Don't think in terms of a chair or a sofa or a style. Think broader. Think feeling.

Feelings are your best indicators and unveil your true self.

I recommend that you gather images that are not even related to interior décor, in order to keep your mind unfettered by interior design. In other words, peruse travel magazines, pop culture, anything that interests you, because once you select an image, for example, of an ad for Napa Valley, you may love the feeling that this area evokes, or the colors of the greenery, or it might inspire a wine cellar. Whatever the reason for the selection, it is very personal and should be done with a very open mind.

If you see an image in a travel magazine—let's use the example we used earlier of Tuscany—you see the interior of a villa, and it makes you smile and makes you feel happy, that's an image you should grab. If you can see yourself in that space, you want to use it for your dream board.

A perfect example is a dear friend who loves warm colors. All of her color selections are warm hues. *Under the Tuscan Sun* is her favorite movie. That's what her dream house looks like. These inspirations may eventually translate into a piece of furniture, but for now it's about the feelings that will lead to inspired living.

You are free to use whatever method you prefer to create your board; however, I highly recommend you create an actual board, whether digital or pin-up. The reason for this is that you want the images some place where you can stand away from them and look at them as a whole **collage** of sorts. Hopefully you can find a place to save your dream board for continued inspiration, because as you go on the rest of this journey, you're going to want to look back at it. This way, you will see that the blend of the images start to come together as a whole expression of your vision.

So once you have chosen the images, you want to tune in and be aware of what you like about them.

You want to ask yourself questions about each image to understand what exactly you like about it, just like my client who loved the color of the flowers versus the entire room.

Here are some of the questions you will want to ask of yourself and if you feel inspired, jot your answers down in the "pause to reflect" page at the end of this chapter.

1. "What really stands out for me in this image?"

2. "How does this room or space make me feel?"

3. "How do I imagine myself using this _____
(Fill in room, space, color, material, etc…)

4. "What item in this room represents me and why?"

5. "What emotions would I use to describe this image?"
(Relaxed, exciting, refreshing, etc…)

6. "What activity does this room represent that I would love to experience?"

7. "How do I imagine myself in this image?"

As you ask yourself these questions and discover what moves you, you are going to want to keep the answers in what I call a dream board diary in order to become clearer about each image. Think of it like writing captions for your ideal lifestyle. Don't get caught up in the answers; single words are just as good for this purpose. All of these steps are here for a very specific reason. Your dream board and diary will serve as a tangible reference, and as so many of my clients have found, it's fun to have your own personal photographic portfolio of taste, desire, and lifestyle.

It is important when creating your sacred spaces that you use your reference images, and when it's time to go shopping for the actual pieces, you will feel less overwhelmed and avoid choosing the wrong things. If you skip this step, you won't have a visual reference of images that reflect your desires. You need the dream board images and the understanding that comes from answering the questions. By asking yourself questions and answering them in an honest and clear way, you are literally creating your lifestyle—one word, image, and answer at a time. Believe me, as you evolve to the next more concrete steps of the process, these abstract ideas will allow the physical aspects of your interiors to unfold in a very real way, with a new and specific purpose, resonating with *who you are* in a way that was not previously explored. They will create the foundation for your enlightened design.

Once you have completed your dream board, you will keep referring to it as you go through the additional steps in creating your sacred spaces. Later on when you see a piece you like, this board and insight will empower you to know with greater certainty if this item coincides with your desires or really makes sense with your original vision.

Just because you fall in love with an item doesn't mean it makes sense for your lifestyle. This is the guidance that I often offer my clients that you will be able to do for yourself with the foundations you have created with these first two steps. Many times, with their dream board images in mind, I am able to pose questions to a client when I see them gravitating toward a piece of furniture, a particular color, or a specific layout that doesn't jive with the original inspirations they started with. I will ask, "Does that really match the vision you originally had for that room?" Or, "You mentioned that comfort is important to you. Does that chair seem comfortable enough for you?" Even a consistent color that reveals itself in most of their images is easy to spot when you see them gathered together on an inspiration board—which brings me to a topic that I'm excited to dive into becuase it is often a trigger for our deepest emotions.

COLOR

When looking at your dream board, you might have noticed that their is a particular color that consistently stands out or becomes repetitive in most of your images. This is because *color* is one of the most significant and emotionally charged elements influencing design. Similarly, when guiding my clients, I find that color is usually what they are the most clear about. Color is such a wonderful design element, especially because it is so subjective and personal, and although there are hundreds of books regarding this topic that cover theories and principles, I will address just some of the basics of color to assist you in refining your personal preferences. As you select the images for your dream board, make sure to make a note on any particular color that "feels right" or attracts you, because it will help inspire you as you create your sacred spaces.

Color can be the most exciting, inspirational, and transformative aspect influencing your sacred space. This topic is usually the one that is most easily offered as a preference when initiating a room's design. There are so many types of color schemes, however, that evaluating them from an academic perspective can sometimes be a bit overwhelming for a person that is not in the field of design. At the end of the day, how you feel about a particular color or color scheme is very personal and as varied as there are personalities.

With a few helpful tips, you will feel more empowered in making the decisions that can help acquire the desired effect and emotional response you are striving for. Even though there truly is no wrong or right scheme, the best rule of thumb to keep in mind is that in color, as in design, an underlying sense of order is generally satisfying, and although there are standard color schemes that are nothing more than time-tested recipes, rarely do actual textbook color schemes fit perfectly into a particular category.

What I recommend is to use your dream board process to become aware of what you are drawn to as well as the descriptions of your questionnaire to help you determine your tolerances and preferences regarding color. What I have found helpful as I develop a color scheme for my clients is to ask, "Is there any particular color you don't like?" This always offers the most insight into the absolute no-no's of color for you.

Although generalizations are often risky, the following principles tend to hold true:

- *Warmer, stronger, or more contrasting colors create an active and stimulating environment.*

- *Cooler, neutral, or generally harmonious colors, create a more relaxed and calming environment.*

The reason I mention *warmer* versus *cooler* is because each hue has its own *temperature* that affects our spaces in a particular way and with a new awareness can be used to our advantage in establishing a personally satisfying color scheme.

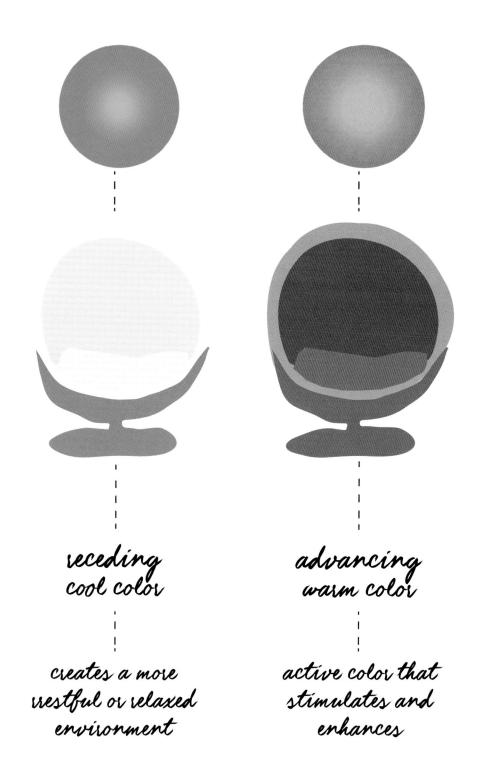

*receding
cool color*

*creates a more
restful or relaxed
environment*

*advancing
warm color*

*active color that
stimulates and
enhances*

The warmer the color (think of the sun), such as red, orange, and yellow, the more active it is, and therefore it is called an *advancing color*. These colors seem to be coming toward us or appear nearer to us when used on walls or other objects. The use of this warm advancing color on larger objects, such as on an upholstered sofa, can give the appearance that the piece is larger than it truly is. By contrast, cooler colors (think of the water), such as blue, violet, and green, have the opposite effect and are considered *receding colors*. They can be selected to create a more restful or relaxed atmosphere within a space. When purposely used, these colors can create a desired experience in a space.

The *value* of a color, or its lightness and darkness, can also be an influencing factor in order to maximize its advancing or receding effects. Many people make the common assumption that selecting a darker shade of a particular color will make a space appear smaller, when often I have found the opposite to be true, especially when the color temperature of the color is taken into account. A dark navy blue wall will usually enlarge a room, while a bright red wall will visually reduce the space, making the wall appear closer. Keep these very basic concepts in mind when selecting color for your sacred spaces in order to achieve the desired effects that will influence how you feel in your home.

Another basic yet important lesson to apply is that color schemes fall into two major categories, *related* and *contrasting*. The way we determine this is the relationship of each color on the color wheel. A color wheel is a circle that is divided in twelve equal sections that shows the relationships of each color according to its pigment and *color value.*

This tool shows the relationship between colors. Being that all colors are created from the three *primary* colors (red, blue, and yellow), this wheel allows you to see each color as it relates to the others. The main purpose for this information is to help you understand concepts of how colors are *related* or *contrasting*, as mentioned above. *Related*—also known as *analogous*—color schemes are made up of one or more colors next to each other on the color wheel, which generally leads to more harmony and a general feeling of unity. *Contrasting* —also known as *complementary*— colors are based on colors that are opposite to each other on the wheel. These color schemes offer a greater variety and balance between cool and warm hues. They are very different but not necessarily better or worse than the other.

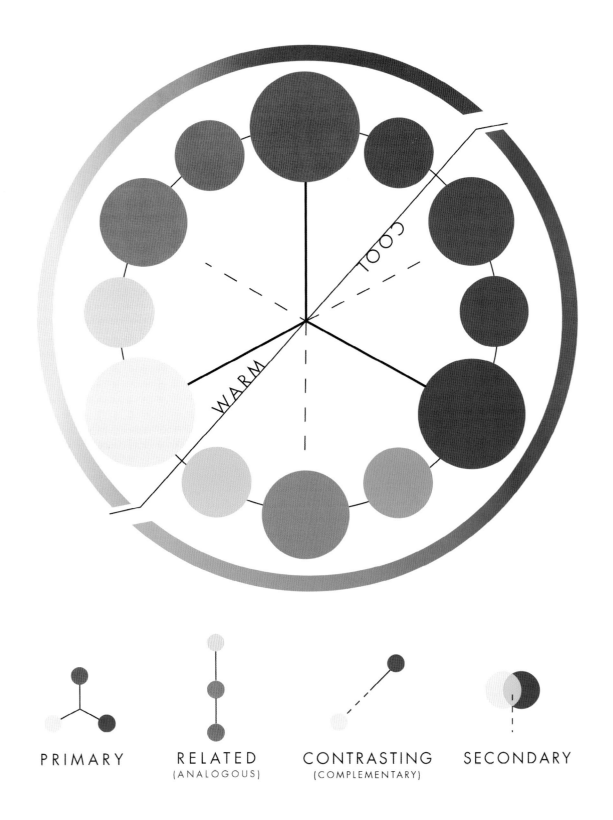

PRIMARY

RELATED
(ANALOGOUS)

CONTRASTING
(COMPLEMENTARY)

SECONDARY

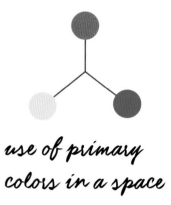

use of primary colors in a space

As you look at the images on this page, you might be drawn to one or the other, and this can help you become clearer about your personal preference. The key factor here is that this is meant to create *clarity* and awareness in you, since, as I mentioned, there is no wrong or right preference. Just follow your gut instincts and let feelings be your guide. You might even prefer a combination of color relationships or be inspired to use different ones for different rooms. I have found that one of the most commonly preferred schemes is to have a neutral or harmonious foundation for walls, ceilings, and floors and then add color through art and accessories, giving a very flexible and livable strategy that allows for the many people that will use the spaces.

So now we have a solid footing, a strong foundation, and clear purpose to help bring the next steps to fruition. I'm so excited to see the rest unfold for you, and unfold it will. In the next chapter, we will start to evaluate room functions and start dealing with room sizes and real furniture, and pretty soon our sacred spaces will become a reality.

use of related/analogous in a space

use of contrasting/ complementary colors in a space

Los Angeles Loft by
Mae Brunken Designs

REVIEW OF TERMS

ABSTRACT

Relating to or involving general ideas or qualities rather than anything specific.

AUTHENTIC

Of undisputed origin; geniune. Not false or copied; real.

COLLAGE

An assemblage of different images placed together to form a new whole.

ADVANCING COLOR

Usually a pure, strong, warm or hot color that visibly comes forward to the eye.

RECEDING COLOR

Any various cooler colors that tend to appear farther from the eye.

COLOR VALUE

The relative darkness or lightness of a color.

CLARITY

Clearness as to perception or understanding;
freedom from indistinctness or ambiguity.

Dreaming and Exploring Color

Picking out Beautiful Images and Exploring our Preferences through Them

They say that a picture is worth a thousand words, and in this step, that could not be truer. In this chapter, you learned to select images that visually represent your dreams and hopes for yourself in your home. Just as the story of my client loving the color of the flowers as her greatest influence, the subtle nuances within each image are personal to you and will therefore conjure emotions that will keep you on track and aligned. It is my hope that this second step evokes the emotions in you that will lead to this.

"All human beings are dream beings. Dreaming ties all mankind together."

—Jack Kerouac

pause to reflect

"I give you
permission
to USE
YOUR
ROOMS"

CHAPTER 4

STEP 3 — PERMISSION GRANTED

Tools

Bubble Diagram

Enlightenment

Achieve Outside-the-Room Thinking

Freedom … doing what you want, where you want, when you want, with whom you want. That's what this chapter is about. It's a hall pass. It's *Ferris Bueller's Day Off*.

The freedom to do things the way we truly want, and not the way we are conditioned by our experiences growing up or the influences of designs from the past, is a matter of awareness. Without even being conscious of it, we are accustomed to *using* the rooms in our homes the way they were established by some higher authority, whether it's the way the architect established it, or the builder, or maybe even the way we were told by the realtor that showed us the house in the first place. Either way, what I have found is that we accepted the labels presented to us for the uses of these rooms as a given, without questioning whether they are best suited for our needs. Well, I am here to present a new concept, one that is based on total freedom—freedom to use these rooms as we see fit for our personal lifestyles. In other words, I give you permission to *use* your rooms.

There have been so many examples during my career in which I've used what I call design therapy to help my clients rethink their conditioned beliefs in a way that makes room for their authentic lives.

A perfect example of this is when I sat with clients that enjoy learning and playing musical instruments, and they all practice their instruments separately, but secretly they longed to play and enjoy music as a family. As I asked them some exploratory questions and used a little of my *design therapy,* I began to see that all of them loved playing music as well as the idea of having a place to play music together. I looked around and saw that they had a really large living room complete with the typical living-room-like furniture: a large sofa, coffee table, and so on. I promptly suggested dedicating the living room for their communal, musical enjoyment. "Let's make the living room the music room!" I said excitedly. Well, their first reaction was, "We can't do that! What would our guests think?" The next logical question was, "How often do you spend time with guests there?" They answered, embarrassed, "Never." So, I asked, "Why wouldn't you want to make this a music room then? What's so bad about that?" Almost immediately, I saw a smile of acceptance come to their faces as they recognized how silly they had been to not think of this themselves. "Yeah, let's put the piano in there, and let's bring the bar in … and let's do everything in chairs and no sofas. Why do we need a sofa? Nobody sits in the sofa. Everybody can be gathered around listening to us play music instead," they said. And so the transformation began. This once-neglected living room turned into the music room lounge, a place where not only the family came together to enjoy making music but where guests were invited to come in and join the fun, with microphones added for singing.

Another eye-opening example was when I walked into a beautiful condominium apartment that was located directly on the water. It was for a preliminary consultation. During my initial review and assessment with the client, I became very aware that something was truly out of whack. As we walked through the many rooms of the apartment, I saw an elegantly furnished living room and dining room, a lavishly appointed study, which looked perfect, so perfect in fact that it begged the question, in my mind of course,

I wonder if these rooms are used.

As I looked closer, I saw a tiny plastic toy oven and all the paraphernalia that accompanies a well-appointed playroom in the dining room! Deeper still into the rooms of the condo, I saw that there was a small paper-filled desk in the corner of the master bedroom, and it was quite obviously being used. The client apologized profusely to me for these design faux pas and gave me all kinds of excuses for the grave offenses that she had supposedly committed. She continued to explain how she was studying for her master's degree while raising six-year-old twins. I thought this scenario to be one of the most ironic I had ever seen of misalignment. There were clearly several rooms of very grand size with waterfront views, no less, available for claiming and using, and here was this amazing, intelligent woman apologizing and hiding her authentic life in corners.

Once realizing this, I asked her why she wasn't using the study to study or the living room to live in, and she wasn't able to give me an answer that made any sense. She simply said she hadn't thought of it because those rooms were "supposed to be perfect."

I couldn't help asking her, "Perfect for whom? Those who don't live here?" Needless to say, she looked at me like I had three heads, but after another hour of design therapy, we wound up moving her things into the study and combined the dining room with the living room so that the girls could freely play in the space without being ashamed.

DESIGN
ENLIGHTENMENT
MOMENT

We are heavily conditioned by our past experiences, the ones we grew up with, the customs of our parents, and even our peers, and we forget to give ourselves the opportunity to *think differently.*

I also encouraged her to use her breakfast table to play games by bringing it closer to the seating arrangement where most of her family gathered, something she confessed was a mission because the coffee table was always too low and the games were so difficult to get out of storage. By the time I left, she clearly looked as transformed as the rooms we had rearranged. Her demeanor was lighter, happier, and remarkably contented.

Now, as I tell this story, it may either seem ridiculously obvious that the solutions where right in front of her, or you may see yourself in a similar predicament. I find that sometimes, the things that are often right in front of us are the ones we have the hardest time seeing, until of course, something or someone makes us aware of it.

I hope that this book brings awareness to the habits in your life that might be hard for you to see. We are heavily conditioned by our past experiences, the ones we grew up with, the customs of our parents, and even our peers, and we forget to give ourselves the opportunity to *think differently.*

So, I have a question for you. An important one.

When was the last time you dined in your formal dining room?

Usually when I ask my clients this question, the most common answer is, "Thanksgiving."

Have you ever asked yourself why that is? Why do we designate a room that takes up so much space to be used only once or twice a year? Is it because it's too much of a hassle to bring food into it, or maybe it's because we don't feel relaxed in that setting, or maybe we simply think that it's not *supposed* to be used daily. For whatever reason, **the dining room has become the least dined in, and the living room the least lived in.** The very concept of these rooms and their formal labels seems to be a remnant from the past when in some ideal world we had butlers and servants that set the table formally, and we lived a fantasy represented by those fairy tales. In this fantasy, we dressed up for dinner, and everything was beautifully arranged for us. Really? How crazy is this?

The same thing has happened to our living rooms. This room, which I call the least lived in, has become abandoned. It's also not serving our present lifestyles and, in turn, is often a neglected space. It's as if we need this room as the curtain of perfection for Oz to hide behind.

I say we pull back the curtain and let our true lives embrace these spaces in whatever way we choose to.

At this moment, I can almost palpably feel the ***resistance*** from those of you reading this concept as absurd. This concept of *using* our rooms is almost as taboo as sex in public spaces.

Analyzing what activity will bring life back into these rooms is the step in your transformational process that will revive these abandoned rooms and fulfill these deserted desires.

Maybe during the questionnaire you discovered that playing Monopoly and Scrabble was a favorite pastime when you were a kid. And you have asked yourself,

"Why don't I do that now?"

Your answer may be, "Because I don't really have a place to play Scrabble and God forbid we should *play* in the formal dining room!"

I say, let's erase *should* from our vocabulary and blow room bubbles unabashedly with childlike freedom.

I have adapated a tool from design school called the **bubble diagram** to create a simple and fun way of discovering which rooms you should enjoy these activities in.

This fun and easy method allows you to assign each room with a function, without the limitations of the room labels you are accustomed to and without preconceived notions.

Go ahead. I give you permission to use your rooms!

Why bubbles? Because we are not ready for walls or the boundaries that walls create.

How do we do this? Well, the best way to answer that question is to show you an example.

On the next page you will find a traditional bubble diagram and the floor plan it inspired.

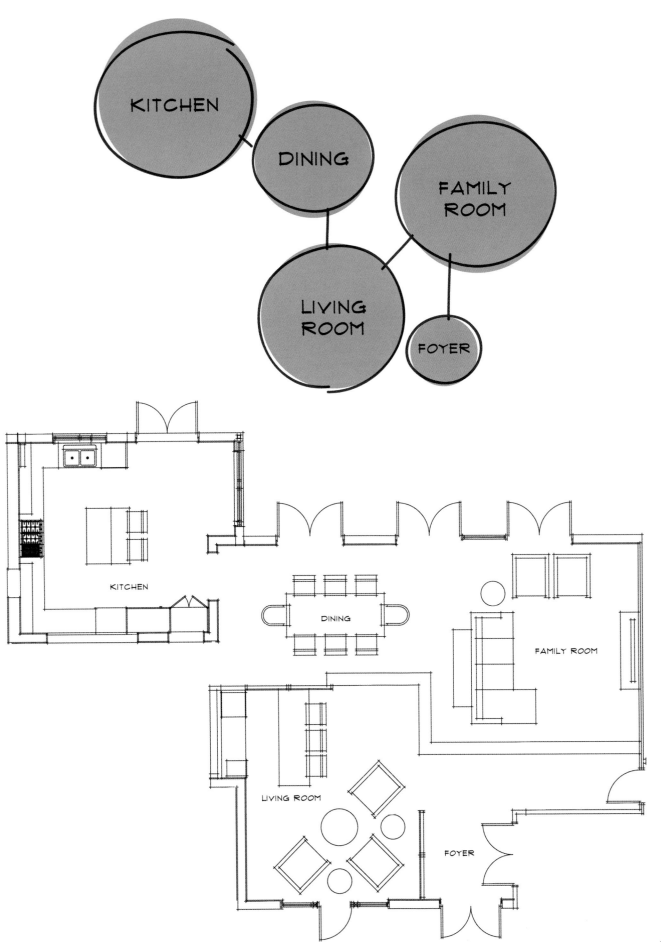

KITCHEN

DINING

FAMILY ROOM

LIVING ROOM

FOYER

KITCHEN

DINING

FAMILY ROOM

LIVING ROOM

FOYER

Originally, the bubble diagram was used by the designer or architect as a precursor to the basic floor plan. Its main purpose was to help establish logical adjacencies between the rooms. For our purposes, however, the bubbles will hold the activities you currently do as well as the activities you wish to do.

Here is an example of my version already filled in for your reference.

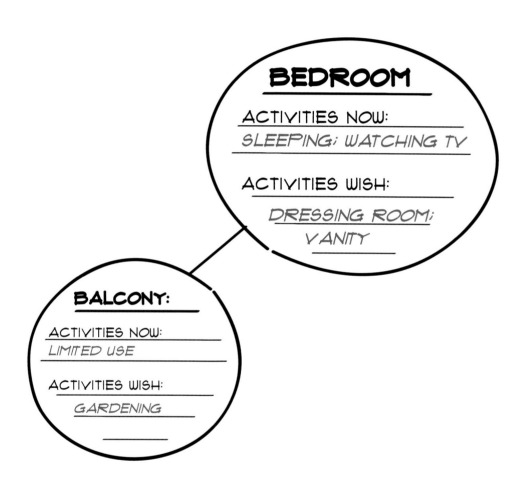

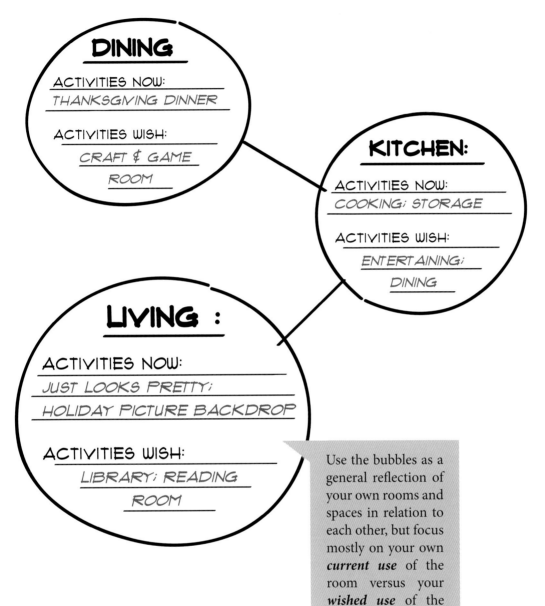

DINING

ACTIVITIES NOW:
THANKSGIVING DINNER

ACTIVITIES WISH:
CRAFT & GAME
ROOM

KITCHEN:

ACTIVITIES NOW:
COOKING; STORAGE

ACTIVITIES WISH:
ENTERTAINING;
DINING

LIVING :

ACTIVITIES NOW:
JUST LOOKS PRETTY;
HOLIDAY PICTURE BACKDROP

ACTIVITIES WISH:
LIBRARY; READING
ROOM

Use the bubbles as a general reflection of your own rooms and spaces in relation to each other, but focus mostly on your own ***current use*** of the room versus your ***wished use*** of the room or space.

This exercise is what I like to call "thinking outside the room." We can sort out the logistics later as the actual floor plan and space planning take shape in the next chapters.

The bubbles help you map out the activities you want without getting stuck in a room that doesn't fulfill your true desires and expectations. Doesn't that make sense?

I believe we begin to experience this disconnect when we go furniture shopping. We walk into a store, and what do we see? Room *settings*—the living room set, dining room set, or bedroom set—that create a preconceived idea of what these spaces should be. These settings present a generic lifestyle as imagined by a furniture manufacturer rather than a personalized layout catered to your unique lifestyle.

So I encourage you to **think outside the room***, and outside of the room setting, and to not get caught up in* **how** *you're supposed to live and* **who** *you're supposed to be but rather to honor your desires and the* **individuality** *of your life.*

Every one of us comes with an incredible amount of self-worth and expression, and being authentic is part of that. With something that seems as innocent as furniture, we can get caught up in the pretension of being something we're not, and suddenly our interior spaces have nothing to do with who we are.

If our home doesn't represent who we truly are, then how can we live as our authentic selves? I believe our homes have been created without a true awareness of who we are or what we want to be and do.

DESIGN
ENLIGHTENMENT
MOMENT

I emphasize here that there is no wrong or right way to express ourselves in our rooms and that it is time to ask the right questions of ourselves and reevaluate our conditioned beliefs about how we want to live.

Let me give you some examples of ideas that can help you get started. Maybe you live alone and really enjoy hanging out in your bedroom and having a place to have a cup of tea, but a bed doesn't support that. Why not set up an area in the bedroom where you can do that? Sounds simple, right? This is the freedom I am talking about when adding an activity to a space and *thinking outside the room*.

These functions and activities are going to be the essence of what you and your family's environment and gatherings are going to be set around, because *you've* created them ***consciously***. Let's break the boundaries of our rooms and liberate our thoughts about them. This is why I love the bubbles exercise—because the limiting beliefs created by our walls are set free.

There is no wrong or right way to express ourselves in our rooms and it is time to ask the right questions of ourselves and reevaluate our conditioned beliefs about how we want to live.

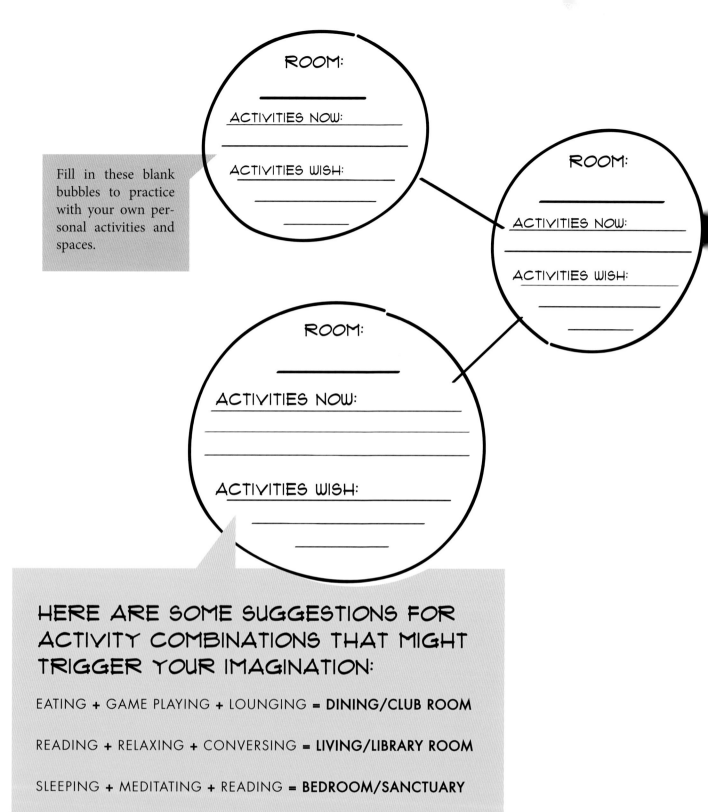

ROOM:

_____

ACTIVITIES NOW:
_____
_____

ACTIVITIES WISH:
_____
_____

ROOM:

_____

ACTIVITIES NOW:
_____
_____

ACTIVITIES WISH:
_____
_____

Fill in these blank bubbles to practice with your own personal activities and spaces.

ROOM:

_____

ACTIVITIES NOW:
_____
_____
_____

ACTIVITIES WISH:
_____
_____

HERE ARE SOME SUGGESTIONS FOR ACTIVITY COMBINATIONS THAT MIGHT TRIGGER YOUR IMAGINATION:

EATING + GAME PLAYING + LOUNGING = **DINING/CLUB ROOM**

READING + RELAXING + CONVERSING = **LIVING/LIBRARY ROOM**

SLEEPING + MEDITATING + READING = **BEDROOM/SANCTUARY**

GAMES + WATCHING TV + ENTERTAINING = **FAMILY/CLUB ROOM**

READING + MEDITATING +WORKING = **STUDY/OFFICE**

EXERCISING + MEDITATING + WORKING = **GYM/HOME OFFICE**

CRAFTING + GARDENING + READING = **TERRACE/BALCONY**

Here's the list that you filled out in chapter 2 in your discovery questionnaire to remind you of your desired activities. It might be fun to compare your previous answers to see if they have changed or remained consistent. Your goal is to give your spaces a new purpose that truly aligns wth your lifestyle.

☐ PLAYING INSIDE   ☐ DANCING

☐ PLAYING OUTSIDE   ☐ EXERCISING

☐ GARDENING   ☐ RELAXING

☐ READING   ☐ SOCIALIZING

☐ SINGING   ☐ EATING

☐ CRAFTING   ☐ BATHING

☐ STUDYING   ☐ DRAWING/PAINTING

☐ CONVERSING   ☐ COOKING

☐ PLAYING MUSIC   ☐ ENTERTAINING

☐ LISTENING TO MUSIC   ☐ BUILDING

☐ WATCHING TV/MOVIES   ☐ NAPPING/SLEEPING

☐ ROLE PLAYING/ACTING   ☐ OTHER:

☐ WORKING

If you have the luxury of space in the way of extra square footage and can dedicate a single activity to a room, by all means feel free to allow yourself that treat. The fewer activities each individual room has, the simpler it will be to furnish the room later on. Keep in mind, however, that more space doesn't necessarily mean more function. What is truly important here is to make sure that all of your desires are accounted for from the earlier exercises in the questionnaire and dream board. Go back and review your answers. Create a check list if you must, but make sure you've covered your *activity* bases.

Because an activity literally activates a room.

Of course, there might be other activities that can be added according to your personal preferences in time. In my case, for example, I had the luxury of converting a room into my personal ballet studio, a dream that I had for many years that didn't come about until my children had grown up and left home. This brings up a very interesting point regarding our homes and the lives we lead in them.

We are always expanding and evolving, and we can continue to use this process in the future when our needs change and our living requirements evolve.

I am excited by what I see already happening in our workspaces or commercial spaces, such as areas that intentionally promote privacy or areas that encourage collaboration and even play. These shifts in thinking have begun to transform the way our work environments are being designed, but these concepts are lagging behind in the home.

We can create our homes anew and fully embrace every square inch as long as we give ourselves permission to **think outside the room.**

Let's HEAL OUR HOMES with new ideas about space, rooms, and functions and in the process HEAL OUR LIVES.

RESISTANCE

The forces that counteract progress.

SET OR SETTINGS

A manipulated grouping.

The context and environment in which something is created.

INDIVIDUALITY

The quality or character of a particular person or thing
that distinguishes them from others.

CONSCIOUSLY

In a deliberate and intentional way.

ASSIGNMENT
ENLIGHTENMENT

CHAPTER RECAP

Permission Granted

*Go Ahead
Use Your Rooms and Play*

I hope creating your room bubbles was fun! In this chapter, you learned to *think outside the room* instead of accepting preconceived room labels. You also had the freedom and liberty to assign activities to each room as you saw fit. Your life and your rooms are yours and step by step will clearly reflect who you are and the life you wish to lead. How liberating is that?

"The key to organizing an alternative society is to organize people around what they do, and more importantly what they want to do."

—Abbie Hoffman

pause to reflect

"often times
it is about
HOW A
SPACE
FEELS"

CHAPTER 5
STEP 4—REAL SPACE PLANNING

Tools
Actual Floor Plans

Enlightenment
Master True Scale, Proportion, and Layout

A s an interior designer with over thirty years of practical experience, I have been blessed to work on so many spaces. Large, grand-scale, open ones to tiny, compact ones, and each one has presented unique perspectives and challenges that have led to satisfying transformations. The reason I bring this up is because the beauty of a space is truly in the eyes and beliefs of the beholder, just like the old adage. Design is so subjective, and wrongs or rights are really about appropriateness for each individual's needs and this more about *interpretation* versus correctness. I have experienced a degree of restful respite in the smallest of rooms and just as readily have experienced anxiety and stress in the grandest.

If you ever walk into a room, and it doesn't quite feel right or there is an apparent awkwardness to the functions within it, scale and proportion could very well be the culprit for this. Why this may be occuring and guidelines for outfitting a room are two of the many things we will cover in this chapter.

In order to be successful at this, you need to first understand the concept of **scale.** So, for example, If I'm standing next to my friend Magita, a six-foot Swedish blonde, we're like Danny DeVito and Arnold Schwarzenegger, since I'm a five-foot, petite-framed woman. Relative to each other, I appear tiny, and she appears large. But if I'm standing next to my friend Alice, who is closer to my size and frame, *we're* **proportionate** or *in scale* to each other. In simple terms, everything's size is relative to everything else's size.

my dear Swedish friend, Magita, and me looking like Arnold Schwarzenegger and Danny DeVito in "Twins"

my friend Alice and me, side by side, as proportionately petite Latinas

It's how a grape appears in size next to an apple. Or how a watermelon appears next to an orange. How this relates to spacial arrangements is a very important factor in design. Capturing the correct scale and proportion for a room's elements can make all the difference. Especially when it comes to adding the furniture.

For instance, a really big sofa in a very tiny room, scale-wise, might look off. I'm not saying that sometimes rules of scale can't be broken, but usually the best-designed spaces have a great relativity of scale, which translates into a great feeling space.

Another factor that needs to be considered is **circulation space** required for **foot traffic**. The biggest mistake people make is that they forget to think about the "negative space" of a room or furniture configuration—in other words, how people will get through the spaces and around the furniture.

So many times I have reviewed a floor plan created by an architect without any furniture drawn into each room. At first glance, the rooms appear to be suitable or appropriately sized for the intended purpose, however, without the furniture drawn in, the amount of usable space can be deceiving. Without the furniture it's challenging for anyone to visualize themselves in a room and understand what really fits. It's the furniture that allows us to imagine walking through a space and therefore reveals the circulation or negative space that a room must have for it to function and flow. In the following diagrams you will see the awkwardness created by the doorways that are traversing the usability of the room.

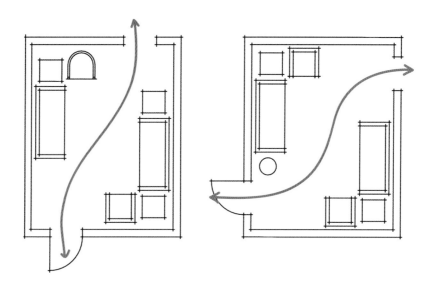

UNDESIRABLE CIRCULATION
Traffic interrupts seating arrangement
producing less interaction.

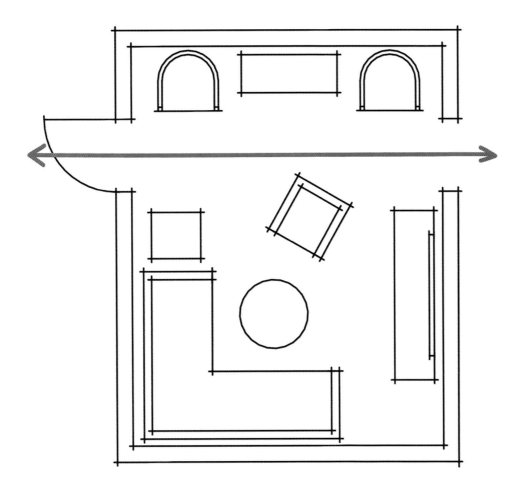

GOOD CIRCULATION
Traffic is direct and does not cut across
main seating area maximizing interaction.

To recap, it's clear that you want good balance and proportion, and in order to achieve this you will need to play close attention to the sizes of things in relation to each other or just remember my "fruity" example I helped you visualize earlier in the illustration. It will also involve measuring your spaces and furniture carefully in order to gauge how they are relative to each other. A good way of doing this is to use the spaces and furniture you live in now with this new awareness of scale. Once you start seeing things with these concepts in your mind, you will soon become conscious of scale in making choices.

In order to get started we must create a **floor plan.** *A scaled* **floorplan** *and* **furniture layout** *is of the greatest importance. It will help you not only to visualize the room's functions, but it will serve as a guide for all of the next steps in realizing the completion of your sacred spaces.*

Ideally, if you have a floor plan that already exists, given to you by the architect or developer of your home, it will save you the time in creating one from scratch. However, in the event that you don't have one, I will take you step by step through the process of creating one. I can't emphasize enough how important a scaled working floor plan is. Once the basic plan is created, we will continue to add the furniture until we have a functional working space plan and, more importantly, one that aligns with your true lifestyle.

If you already have a floor plan from your architect, the standard scale used in reading and using this plan is in quarter inch scale, meaning that one quarter inch is equal to one foot. Most floor plans are created in this scale, and therefore we will use this scale to create ours if one is not available. What this scale means, in simple terms, is that for every quarter inch on a ruler, the equivalent is equal to one foot, or twelve inches.

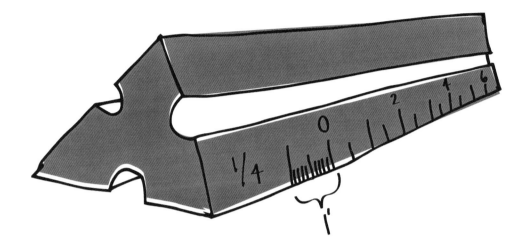

Scaled Architectural Ruler

The scaled architectural ruler is the tool that helps us see each quarter inch individually, using the quarter-inch section of the ruler in which each line of the quarter inch represents one foot.

I must note that there are numerous online tools for creating floor plans, and if you are so inclined, feel free to use them in order to create a plan. These programs often have furniture **templates** that can facilitate the process of adding furniture to your floor plan. However, if you've opted to go the old-fashioned way, using paper and pencil (this is still my favorite), I will teach you the basics of creating a floor plan step-by-step. You will also have access to an online video tutorial accessible to you through the purchase of this book.

ONLINE TOOLS

1. Home Styler
2. Roomsketch
3. Planning Wiz

APPS FOR SMARTPHONES

1. Home Design 3D (iOS), Free and $6.99
2. Floor Plan Creator (Android), Free
3. MagicPlan (iOS), Free
4. Inard Floor Plan (Android), Free
5. Room Planner by Chief Architect (iOS), Free

**The following are the tools to acquire
in order to create your basic floor plan:**

Quarter-Inch Gridded Paper

The purpose of the gridded paper is to create a floor plan that is
in scale. We do this by assigning each square on the paper the
equivalent of a one-foot-by-one-foot space. So for example, if
your room is ten feet by ten feet, your boundary lines will form a
square that encompasses ten squares by ten squares.

Measuring Tape

The measuring tape will be used to measure rooms as well as any
furniture. Just make sure you get one that has clear markings.
It's preferable for it to have feet and inches defined versus only
inches, as some measuring tapes come with only inch markings,
and this makes it necessary to convert the measurements into feet
and inches for the purpose of our scaled floor plans.

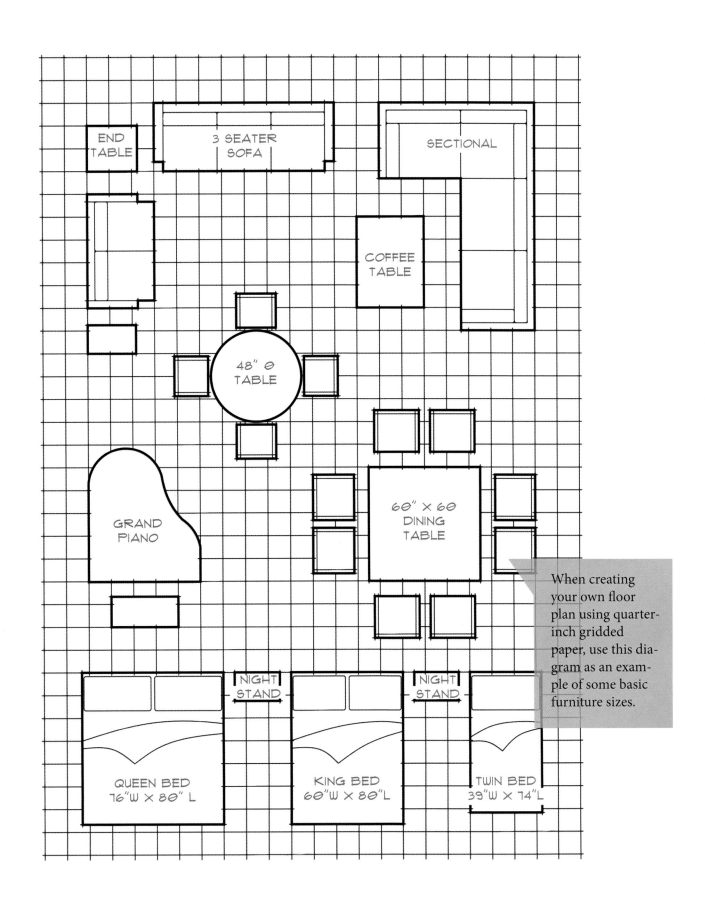

END
TABLE

3 SEATER
SOFA

SECTIONAL

COFFEE
TABLE

48" Ø
TABLE

60" × 60
DINING
TABLE

GRAND
PIANO

When creating
your own floor
plan using quarter-
inch gridded
paper, use this dia-
gram as an exam-
ple of some basic
furniture sizes.

NIGHT
STAND

NIGHT
STAND

QUEEN BED
76"W × 80" L

KING BED
60"W × 80"L

TWIN BED
39"W × 74"L

In order to not become overwhelmed by creating a plan in its totality, you may choose to draw one room at a time. However, if you are daring enough, you can attempt to draw them as they attach to adjacent spaces, such as hallways, corridors, and galleries, as we explored in the bubbles. Adding doors or openings will help to indicate how foot traffic will flow throughout each space, as they serve to demark circulation, which is extremely important for laying out furniture later.

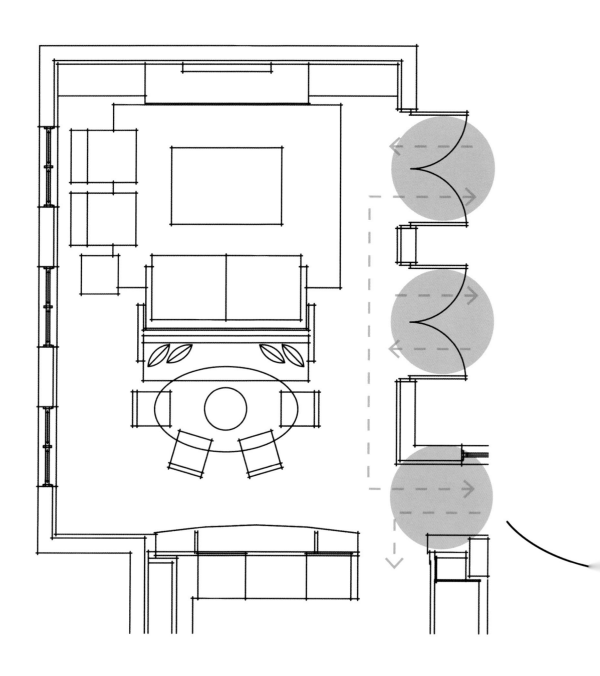

Your floor plans will truly help you to evaluate how much you can fit inside of each space. After you have created your floor plans with whichever method you decide to use, whether paper and pencil or digital, we can get to the fun of filling these rooms with furniture. I assure you that once you are able to draw in and see the furniture in each space, you will get an instant "aha" moment that helps you visualize yourself in the rooms you are creating.

*Remember that **each room will support the functions that you outlined previously in your bubbles** and not necessarily the standard room labels that each room had before. This is an important step to restate that **your life will be integrated into each space and not the other way around**. Each step done without the future anticipation or conditions of the past helps us to build our dream home one room at a time.*

Try not to get ahead of yourself even if you are tempted to start assigning each space. Take your time to leave each room as a generic space and then place within each room the conceptual functions you desire, ultimately supported by the furniture. This next step is when it finally starts coming together, and you will see your wishes and dreams come to fruition within the walls we call home.

Here is an example of a room's layout that combined two functions in a single, compact space—family room and breakfast—allowing the majority of the room to be utilized because foot traffic was minimized to one side of the room.

REVIEW OF TERMS

INTERPRETATION

The action of explaining the meaning of something.

SCALE

A proportion used in determining the dimensional relationship
of one thing against another.

PROPORTIONATE

Relation between things in terms of size,
quantity or number.

CIRCULATION SPACE

The negative space surrounding the positive elements
of a room that allows for appropriate foot traffic or flow.

FOOT TRAFFIC

The flow of people moving in and through a space.

TEMPLATES

Anything that serves as a pattern or mold.

Real Space Planning

*Let's Look at the Real
Spaces in Our Lives*

Now we have begun to make our
dreams and our rooms a bit more
real, even if our activities in them are
about to change and evolve. In this
chapter, you learned how to draw
and assemble your actual rooms
in true scale and size as a building
block for furniture placement and
ultimately your life. This step in the
process is one of the most important
ones and is used as the foundation
for everything else to follow.

"More is not better. Better is better. You don't need a bigger house;
you need a different floor plan. You
don't need more stuff, you need
stuff you'll actually use."

—Alex Steffen

pause to reflect

"and this is where
THE MAGIC
HAPPENS"

CHAPTER 6
STEP 5—PERSONAL FURNITURE LAYOUT

Tools
Scaled Floor Plan and Dream Board Images

Enlightenment
Visualize Each Space as One's Own

I'm so excited to be at this stage of the process with you. We've traveled so far together on this journey of awareness and enlightenment, and we've come to the step that really allows you to see yourself in a space. I have always been fascinated by the many ways in which we can lay out a room. We start with an empty canvas, and these next two stages literally add all of the color to our rooms and our lives.

The awareness that you have gained so far has allowed you to identify who you are and what your dream lifestyle is. In this next step, the placement of furniture will allow you to create the environments that make sense of the open space. Furniture placement is not just about buying the sets that have been sold to us by big-box retailers; furniture is what enables us to live in the spaces we create, and this is where the magic happens.

With this in mind, I will share with you some tips and unconventional ideas that I have learned throughout the years of creating furniture layouts for hundreds of different spaces. The way we place seating in a room truly influences the way in which people behave. We can use some basic principles of layout to support the different uses and interactions that we will have in each room.

Let me explain a few scenarios that will bring this to light. Let's just say that our main intention is to have a much more relaxed and conversation-oriented room. A living room is typically the first one that gets the standard sofa layout, and this is the room that usually gets abandoned first. I have found that without direct eye-to-eye contact with the others in the room, it becomes difficult to be present and engaged in the simple act of conversation. Sometimes I think this is the main reason that cocktail parties purposely keep people standing, becuase in this way, there is no choice but to face each other and talk.

By rethinking the typical furniture layout that is often centered around a sofa, you're going to get a much more **conversational** room. A cozier, more lived-in feeling can be achieved by just changing the furniture layout to allow for people to look at each other. I know that right about now you're saying that this is the first piece of furniture that you think of selecting when furniture shopping for a sitting room, but just think about the body language involved in having a conversation on a sofa. You are either getting a neck ache or twisting into a pretzel. The best conversation-inducing furniture layout is face-to-face, and a sofa is *not* conducive to that.

I have often observed how people behave in sofas. If you don't know each other well, the three-seater sofa is usually perfect for two people. Rarely do you see a three-seater sofa used by three, unless they are family or know each other very well, as in the illustration of The Simpsons on the previous page. If they do venture to pack in the space in the middle, they can barely talk to each other as a group. The truth is, however, that we have been conditioned to select this type of furniture for so long that we don't question it. The two most typical layouts that we are familiar with are based on the sofa as the anchoring piece of furniture in the U or the L-shaped way of arranging furniture.

What usually occurs here is that the two people in the corner are the ones most engaged with each other, because they are the ones closest to being face-to-face. I'm not saying that sofas are not a wonderful piece of furniture. All I'm saying is that the sofa produces a certain type of human behavior that is not necessarily the most conducive to conversation and one-on-one interaction. Sofas are great for other types of activities, such as watching TV or lying down as a single individual.

My favorite layouts for conversation are individual lounge chairs facing each other, gathered around a circular ottoman or table as shown in the following page.

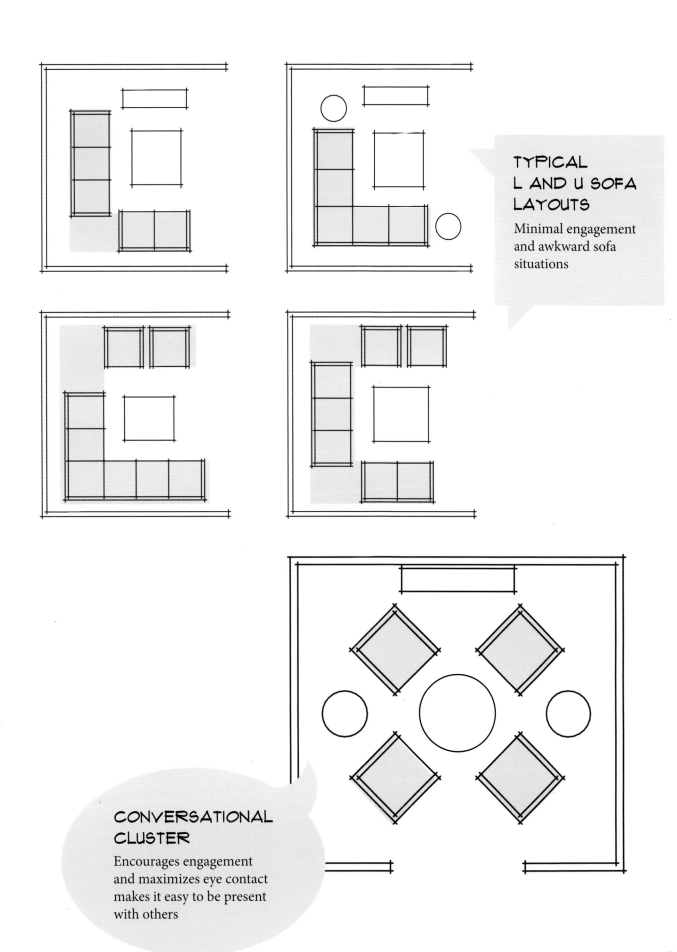

TYPICAL L AND U SOFA LAYOUTS

Minimal engagement and awkward sofa situations

CONVERSATIONAL CLUSTER

Encourages engagement and maximizes eye contact makes it easy to be present with others

Just as the U leads to interaction at the corners, the L does exactly the same thing. As I mentioned before, the four lounge chairs facing each other form more of a circular-shaped layout. Both the circle and the square as a furniture placement layout are my favorites for producing real interaction from people. Which brings me to these two shapes and how they influence the activity of dining.

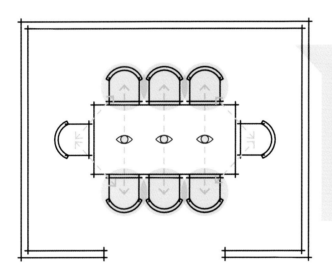

TYPICAL RECTANGULAR DINING TABLE

Lack of eye contact makes conversing and interacting difficult with all diners

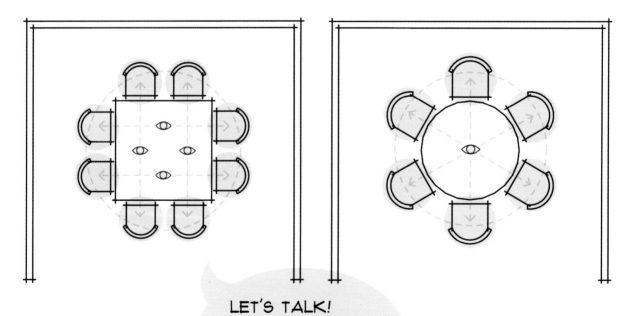

LET'S TALK!

maximize eye contact, interact and converse with ease and comfort

When I moved into my newly built home, I created a beautiful custom-made dining table of my own design, which was a large oval piece of marble. I literally fell in love with the stone and decided it would create a great focal piece for the room. For years, this space was barely used, and when it was, we usually would serve the food, eat, and quite quickly my guests would get up and go to another room to gather and continue the conversations that were being had.

I couldn't figure out why we weren't having lengthy, talkative interactions so typical of Latin dining, a ritual we like to call *sobre mesa* or "over the table." This tradition of lingering over dinner that can last up to three hours was just not happening. At first I thought it might be that the stone was too cold or that the environment was too elegant. After much mental deliberation, I decided to change out my beloved stone table for a different shape. Luckily, my dining room could support my theory in width when I opted for an 80" x 80" square to replace my oval.

Eureka! My theory worked!

My next dinner party became a true success, at least by the standards of my Latin roots. People not only lingered, I ran out of food courses and had to induce them to get up and move to another room.

before

oval table

my previous dining room
design in which nobody
lingered

after

square table

DESIGN
ENLIGHTENMENT
MOMENT

...it is truly important to figure out what your intention is for every room that you are about to lay out, because the furniture layout will be a direct influence in whether the rooms function for that purpose or not.

This is when I discovered that the square or circle allows for sobre mesa or lingering dining room interaction, something that made me, and apparently my guests, really happy.

This is why it is truly important to figure out what your intention is for every room that you are about to lay out, because the furniture layout will be a direct influence in whether the rooms function for that purpose or not. As I mentioned before, the typical room in America is often abandoned for this very reason; the layout is not conducive to the intended activity.

Just as I described in the first chapter how I transformed the way people interacted in my friend's store—before my *furniture layout intervention*—you can do the same with the before and after layouts on the next few pages.

Adjust your furniture and watch what happens.

So if you had a function in your bubble diagram of you and your spouse or friend sitting across from each other and having a cup of coffee and chatting, then you know you will most likely need two chairs and a table to accomplish this. At this phase of the functional furniture layout, you are not trying to pick the type, color, or fabric of the chairs but simply the fact that this particular function needs two chairs and a table. So there's no pressure to choose the exact piece you are going to buy. You're simply choosing the furniture that's going to support your life. Once you have a layout with the furniture you need, you can move forward and start looking for them with the confidence that they will align with the life you truly want and have chosen for yourself.

When I have worked with people in the past and they have been exposed mainly to big box store layouts, sometimes it's difficult to envision what else might be possible. So, on the next few pages you'll find real life examples I've created for my clients to make sure their rooms work for them and that they are truly lived in.

Check out the color coded activity chart to guide you and give you ideas on how you can make your rooms come to life in accordance with your personal lifestyle.

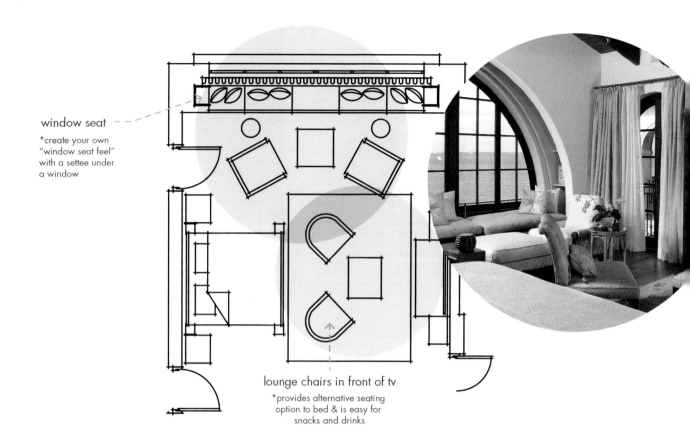

window seat

*create your own
"window seat feel"
with a settee under
a window

lounge chairs in front of tv

*provides alternative seating
option to bed & is easy for
snacks and drinks

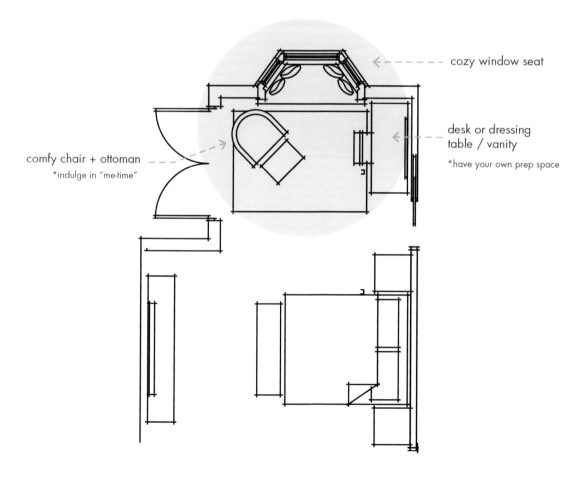

cozy window seat

desk or dressing
table / vanity

*have your own prep space

comfy chair + ottoman

*indulge in "me-time"

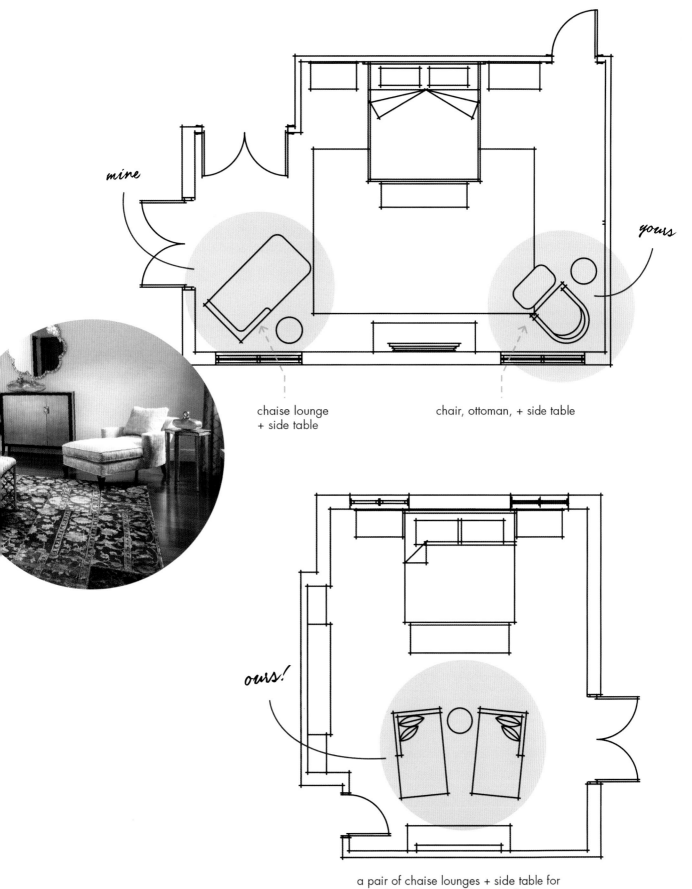

mine

yours

chaise lounge
+ side table

chair, ottoman, + side table

ours!

a pair of chaise lounges + side table for
shared lounging & tv watching

The whole point of this step in the process is that you get to select furniture that supports each space, function, and desire. It is very personal.

Your furniture has to serve YOU, because the purpose of furniture is to support us in the many activities we accomplish, and its shape, size, and proportion play a large role in this primary function.

There are two main proportional directives when it comes to furniture that are very different from each other. These are the scale and size that we are accustomed to, whether we grew up in the United States or Europe. I am not by any means saying that these are the only standards, but for the purpose of this book, the bulk of our familiarity stems from these two main schools of thought when it comes to size and proportion. I like to bring this up because our past conditioning once again heavily influences our personal preferences. European seating, as well as tables and other furnishings, tend to be lower in height and smaller in scale than their American counterparts. The reason this is important is that it is often difficult to blend the two successfully in the same locations. If used together, you may find that one may make the other seem out of scale. The reason for this size difference is mainly based on the sizes of the average home in Europe versus the size of the average American home. This goes back to the relativity in scale that we discussed earlier, and it is valid to mention again. I recommend that when selecting furniture, you pay close attention to seat heights, especially when ordering online through websites, because this is a common mistake.

The typical American seat height is seventeen to eighteen inches, while European seat heights are lower, at anywhere from fourteen to sixteen inches.

It is really amazing what a radical difference these seemingly small amounts are relative to combining furniture as well as comfort levels for different situations.

It is also a good idea to ask yourself what your personal seating height preference is. Use your current furniture as a reference and literally take out a measuring tape and measure the size of the furniture that makes you feel the most comfortable, particularly seat and table heights. Once again, I can't stress enough how personal this is. Time and again I have asked my clients this question in order to be sure I capture their preferences, not just for style but for comfort.

Just in case you're not starting from scratch in this exercise of furnishing your rooms , don't worry — I'm not saying you need to throw everything out. What I am hopefully creating in your mind is a new awareness of how you, your family, and your guests interact in your rooms in response to your furniture layouts.

If you have the typical U shape layout of a sofa and adjacent chairs, try moving them around to face each other or add a couple of small ottomans. You can also look for other pieces in your home that might better serve the activities you desire.

Experiment and have some fun!

REVIEW OF TERMS

CONVERSATIONAL

Conducive of interaction, conversation, and eye contact.

FURNITURE LAYOUT INTERVENTION

My personal design tool in which the belief
"change your layout, change your life" is practiced.

PERSPECTIVE

A particular attitude toward or way of regarding something; a point of view.

ANIMATE

To bring to life.

MINDFUL

To be intentionally conscious or aware of something;
in observation of your thoughts and feelings without judging them as good or bad.

CHAPTER RECAP

Personal Furniture Layout

Make Each Room
Work for You Personally

I hope in this chapter, you've gained some awareness of how much a furniture layout can change things. As we discuss new ways to experience our furniture, we can support our lifestyle and encourage the activities and behaviors we desire within our homes. Go ahead. Try something new and see what happens.

"Design is not just what it looks like and feels like. Design is how it works."

—Steve Jobs

pause to reflect

CHAPTER 7
STEP 6—INDIVIDUALIZED FURNITURE SELECTION

Tools

Websites, Magazines, and Furniture Catalogs

Enlightenment

Furniture Layouts That Really Work for You

And now here we are in the home stretch (pun intended). Now you are ready to go shopping, online or in stores, and select the pieces you want to buy! I have to say, it's also a lot of fun to shop your own furniture with this newfound perspective. So if you already own some pieces with potential, you get to choose those that are going to support you in creating a home that is a true reflection of you. As we transition into this phase of actual selection, begin with those pieces you own first and make choices about where they fit into the new layout you envision for yourself, and then you can add the new pieces that may be missing.

The reason we've waited this long to select the furniture is that up until now we were only selecting in the abstract. Working with the actual floor plan created in scale and with furniture laid out according to our needs and activities we want to experience, we can select from a much more grounded and mindful place. We've learned that the rooms don't necessarily have to have labels; the rooms can be flexible to encompass the different activities that we've taken from our bubble diagram, and it's time to make sure that we have furniture that works with the activities that are going to support them.

We will no longer need to be influenced by the limited layouts of outside sources as the determining factor in our individual furniture selections. What is amazing about the way we find furniture today versus when I started as a designer decades ago is the incredible amount of choices that we have, and we don't even have to go anywhere. We can click our way around the wealth of choices from around the world. As a whole, we are so much more exposed than we have ever been, through websites like Houzz and One Kings Lane.

Escape to JAMAICA

Who wouldn't want to kick off spring with a Caribbean getaway?
We're skipping down to Jamaica's picturesque northern coastline,
home to pristine beaches, ultrachic resorts, and a glamorous literary
legacy. Get into the island spirit and shop the luxe, laid-back look.

Photo by Christian Horan / Island Outpost Images for GoldenEye

MINNA GOODS
The Dash 20 x 20 Pillow II, Gray/Pink

ZOE BIOS CREATIVE
ZBC House Collection, Malta Grass Green

SELAMAT
Bodega 20" Round Side Table, Natural

We quite literally receive dozens of catalogs in our homes on a continuous basis. We are all incredibly familiar with the look of Pottery Barn, West Elm, and Restoration Hardware that present their wares in seductive lifestyle settings. All of these choices are truly amazing, but they can be double-edged swords if we are not aligned with our true selves. The challenge is that by having all of these options we can so easily buy into the pretty pictures that we see because we think we want that life. The life these pictures represent may not **honor** the truth of where we are in our authentic lives.

This is why we have been doing the work. This is why we have been exploring ourselves through this process. I am so happy that through the previous chapters and processes these influences will be seen from a much clearer perspective for you.

*The **dream board** allowed you to visualize some dreams that you've been wanting. The **bubble diagram** allowed you to see the activities that you really desire. Finally, the **furniture layout** on a plan gives you a perfect guideline for how many furniture pieces and what sizes they need to be.*

Between those four steps, you are *empowered* to know what you're looking for. When you walk into a furniture store or pick something out of a catalog ,you will be doing it from the right place, as well as the most knowledgeable place, so that you end up buying furniture that truly suits *your* life and not the fantasy life that may be beautifully presented online or in catalogs.

The first step in actually selecting your furniture is simply to choose the furniture type, one piece at a time. What I mean by this is that this is not the actual pieces that you are going to buy, but rather the *type* of furniture pieces that you have already decided on by placing them on your floor plan, which should also support the particular function in the room you choose. I recommend that you start with the largest piece in the room, because this item becomes the anchor around which all others will stem.

BRAND ALIGNMENT

Just as I mentioned that those big-box images can act as a double-edged sword, they can be used positively with the right guidance. Since these highly marketed brands have embedded there style images into our minds, they can help us when we are starting this step in the *actual* selection process by giving us style guidelines. Take a look at the list here and see which style might resonate with you. Of course these are just a few of the most mainstream brands, as well as a bit more luxury-level brands. It might be helpful to refer back to the list of words you selected to represent your feelings on the earlier chart. The *style* words you selected are helpful here to think about how they tie into the brand names in the list to the right.

These brands connected with your word **associations** will help to get you started in your search for the right pieces of furniture to represent your tastes and lifestyle preferences, thus creating a beautiful alignment once completed.

BRAND ALIGNMENT CHART

Ralph Lauren	Luxurious Americana
Crate & Barrel	Timeless - International
Pottery Barn	Relaxed - Family-Style
West Elm	Earthy - Urban
Restoration Hardware	Streamlined - Historical
CB2	Youthful - Innovative
Ballard Design	Today's Traditional
Z Gallerie	Eclectic Glamour
Anthropology	Bohemian - Artistic
Martha Stewart	Classic Refreshed
Baker	Upscale Transitional
Jonathan Adler	Anti-Depressive Retro
Kartell	Innovative - Modern
Serena & Lili	Nostalgic - Classic
Williams Sonoma	Casual Elegance

Don't stop here! Look for the brands you love and practice your own style associations.

I encourage you to go back to your Dream Board and Discovery Questionnaire and focus on the actual pieces of furniture within the pictures you selected with a new perspective evaluating just the furniture, versus the feelings that the pictures conjured up originally. This may seem redundant to you, since I've mentioned going back to the board several times, but each time we return to our dream board, we focus on different aspects of it. This time we'll go into more detail on furniture style, color, and texture in order to help narrow down our options. If a specific piece seems perfect, then looking into the source information for each item would also be beneficial for you.

I also realize that not everything that you are selecting may be a new purchase; you may have a great deal of furniture that you already own, and depending on a number of different reasons, starting from nostalgia to budget, you may choose to keep or alter them. The wonderful thing about this is that with your new perspectives, you can look at these pieces in a whole new way. It's like shopping your own closets and making a new outfit with the pieces you already own.

Let's shop our own homes and think of every single furniture piece individually.

I have so often come into a client's home even before they have bought anything new and given them a whole new look with what they already own. I find that we are such creatures of habit that we forget to move the chair from one room to another simply because we are so used to it being where it is. This can be so much fun! It truly is one of my favorite activities, and so many of my friends have personally experienced my "*transforming rampages*" during a visit intended just for socializing.

Once you have revisited your dream board with new eyes and are ready to dive into whatever resource is your favorite way of furniture shopping, you will be using your floor plan as a to-do list. Whether you check off each piece on the plan as you find it, like I usually do, or transfer each piece as an item on a list per room, this is important so you don't miss anything.

I also like to draw in or write a list of possible accessories that I would want to complete the room, like a rug, a lamp, or piece of art. In this way, you know the item will be needed to complete your space.

Have fun coloring in your chosen pieces like the example below:

Keep items that you are still searching for highlight free and categorize your items in order of scale and importance.

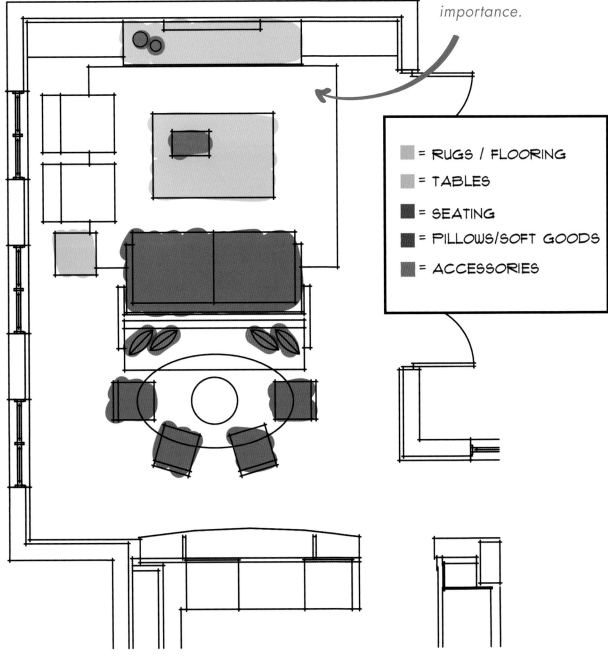

= RUGS / FLOORING

= TABLES

= SEATING

= PILLOWS/SOFT GOODS

= ACCESSORIES

I want to stress how important it is to pick one piece at a time in order to avoid the "big box set" situation. I say this for the reason that we want to make sure we are being authentic in the creation of each space in order to make it sacred and *ours*. In other words, if you need a sofa, look for the sofa. If you need a table, look for the table. If you let yourself go for the whole look, you might end up buying that whole look from one source.

Try to select one by one, without getting ahead of yourself, unless of course you happen to run into a room that completely makes sense for you as it's presented; then by all means go for it. Once again, there's not a wrong or a right here. **It's about making sure you've asked *yourself* the right questions, mostly understanding "why" before fulfilling "what".**

So, let's review some key questions that you want to keep in mind. You might ask,

"Does this fabric, size, comfort level, or position work with my layout and with my lifestyle?"

Though these are very important questions, there is one question that is more important than all of those. And that is,

"How do I feel about this piece of furniture?"

Or,

"How does this furniture make me feel?"

How will you know? Here's the key; focus on feeling.

Ask the "WHY?" before the "WHAT?"

You ask yourself, "How do I *feel* about this piece of furniture?" and then complete that question by seeing if that feeling is in alignment with the original feelings for that room you explored in your chart. If those two things come together, then you've hit the jackpot!

You should get a very quick, instantaneous reaction. And if it makes you smile, then you know that you've connected it. Usually that feeling comes in the first seconds. As I mentioned before, it shouldn't be overthought.

It is very common to think ourselves out of the correct selection instead of following our intuition. And that's where selecting furniture becomes a spiritual practice. It's not just about furniture but rather reading ourselves and making decisions with intention.

You must be *present* with yourself, with your own needs. If you're not present with yourself, you can't be present with your furniture, your families, or your lives. Not being present means you will not feel connected to your home, and others will feel that as well.

So, it's important that as you are looking for the specific item, you're asking yourself the question,

"How do I feel about this chair, and does it align with the feeling that my dream board gave me originally?"

The feelings might be *relaxed, comfortable, glamorous, luxurious, sophisticated, easy, fun,* and *light.* Whichever words and feelings move you.

DESIGN ENLIGHTENMENT MOMENT

You must be present with yourself, with your own needs. If you're not present with yourself, you can't be present with your furniture, your families, or your lives. Not being present means you will not feel connected to your home, and others will feel that as well.

185

my crystals, candles, favorite reading materials & my Angel Cards

Me in my meditation chair

My favorite chair is in my bedroom. I love it because it fits my body just right, and the quiet setting of my bedroom allows me private time away from the noise of the more public areas of my home. I'm very thankful for that chair that makes me want to snuggle into it and read, journal, or meditate—all things that are very important aspects of my lifestyle. We each allow each other to have personal time when we see each other in our chairs. It's almost as if the furniture use communicates the need for this time to each other without the need to express it in actual words.

For us, these things are important, and you can decide what's important for you and be true to that.

This is where establishing priority levels are important when it comes to picking furniture. I would recommend that you decide which items require more of your attention, because not every single thing is going to have the same importance level. You can drive yourself crazy if you make every item equally important. In other words, some pieces of furniture might just be for beauty's sake, and that's perfectly okay.

Having priority guidelines from the beginning will liberate you to enjoy the process of selection much more than stressing out over each and every purchase or decision. You don't have to search the world over for that perfect piece every single time. You also want to leave yourself some wiggle room for things that are there for reasons other than you having picked them out; maybe some of your pieces could have been inherited, which tend to stay in our homes for nostalgia versus function or personal selection.

This reminds me of a story of a really great client of mine. She happened to have inherited a beautiful yet traditional rocking chair that her grandmother left to her. The interesting thing was that she is a modernist, and therefore, her house is very contemporary, but she felt emotionally tied to this very traditional rocking chair.

So, what to do with the rocking chair dilemma? Do you store it away in the attic? Do you hide it in the corner of a rarely used guest bedroom? What do you do?

Here's what we ended up doing. We upholstered it in the coolest Scandinavian fabric, a super bright fabric that gave it an edge. We put it in her family room, and every time she saw it, it would make her smile even though it didn't necessarily "go with" the modern look. That was the perfect solution. We made it look great by refreshing it while keeping the integrity of the original style. It wasn't necessarily a chair she was going to sit in every day. It fit into the category of fun, beauty furniture, and sometimes that's what it's about. It's perfectly okay to have something that is completely impractical but still makes you smile.

In my home, I have so many things that make me smile. I have a lot of objects that I've acquired throughout the years, things that are not necessarily worth a lot of money but that are important to me for other reasons.

One, of course, is my art. I love my art. Even though it's not the most valuable, monetarily speaking, they're all originals, and I love each artist's originality and idiosyncrasies. So that means a lot to me.

My living room is another great depiction of things I have acquired that make me happy. In my living room, I can point out to you four pieces of furniture, maybe five, that I found either in a thrift shop or at a garage sale, and between all of them, I don't think I spent more than $500. And still, every day they bring me joy. Could I replace them with something really fancy or expensive? Sure. Would it make me any happier? No.

So, when it comes to buying furniture, you don't have to do everything store bought either, although a lot of people will tell you differently. But again, that's what this book is about—not listening to others' desires but what's true for you.

Have fun!

pause to reflect

"seemingly
simple items
can bring an
INTANGIBLE
FORCE OF
PERSONAL
NOSTALGIA"

CHAPTER 8
STEP 7 — BEAUTIFYING

Tools
Personal Treasures

Enlightenment
Connect Your Soul to Your Surroundings for Ultimate Spiritual Fulfillment

All of the beautiful rooms we see in the magazines have one thing in common, and it doesn't matter what style they are. They are completely accessorized and styled to add the color and individuality of the particular owner's style and tastes. In actuality, these objects of desire move us emotionally even more than furniture itself. I have often found that these details, the adornments of art, objects, mementos, books, and other ***nostalgic*** items, are what make the difference between spaces that are cold and off-putting into ones that are warm and inviting. Not to mention that the more individualized and personal these objects and collections are, the more character these spaces reflect.

In much the same way that the accessories we add to an outfit can transform a generic look into a personal statement, the details and accessories in a room can make a home go from just good to fabulous. But most importantly, these seemingly simple items can bring an intangible force with them of personal nostalgia that adds an emotional essence as well. Especially when placed in a creative and well-designed way.

By now, you've already set the groundwork for a home in which every space is working to bring the best out in you and those who share it with you. Now that you have the furniture selection that aligns with who you are inside of the spaces that suit your life, the time has come to add the finishing touches that give personality to each area.

This final step could not be more personal. I, myself, have always joked that I can't sleep without being surrounded by books. It's true. I love books! They make me happy. I like picking them up, I like the way they look, and I like the way they make me feel. So in my home you will find books in almost every room. They are my favorite accessories. No matter how digitally advanced we become, I will never get over the pleasure that a beautiful book can bring for me. You may have a similar affinity for other types of objects; I know that art has a similar priority to most of my clients. You may also have collections of objects that bring these feeling out in you.

Baumann Cosmetic and Research Institute
Interior Design by Shulman + Associates
Photography by Emilio Collavino

Beautifying through the use of accessories can turn something that would be considered insignificant into a work of art. A great example can be found in my dermatologist's office. Here is the sleekest, most modern environment, with very *minimalist* furnishings. It's a space that immediately tells the story that they are state-of-the-art dermatologists. However, even in this environment, accessories play a huge role in its beautification. In the lobby, the first thing you see are these acrylic boxes suspended from the walls, filled with antique cosmetic accessories in a museum-like placement—loose powder cases, mirrors, lipstick cases, and all sorts of paraphernalia that were used throughout the ages. All are assembled into a beautiful collection symbolically reminding women of how far cosmetics have come.

So now that you have identified what makes you smile and what you love, you want to identify whether the particular object is something you want where the **public**, such as friends, guests, or visitors, can see it. Or do you want it to be more **private**? For instance, in your bedroom or another room that only you and people close to you will go in?

In my home, in addition to the art that I love *and* that makes me smile, I also have a few personal collections that I have displayed in different ways around my house, some public and some private.

I've been collecting midcentury modern blown glass from my travels for over thirty years. These colorful pieces of glass are not only beautiful but mean something more to me because they all have a history for me.

One of the first vases I purchased was from the first time I went to the Paris Flea Market. I literally brought the vase with me on the plane and held it in my hand in a bag with bubble wrap like a baby on my lap the whole time so that it wouldn't break. All of these are displayed in one place, and every time I look at them, it reminds of everywhere I have traveled. They are all gathered in one vintage unit in my dining room on very public display, with great lighting to enhance all of their various, vibrant colors.

207

I also collect Fu Dogs. They adorn my foyer and live within an antique curio cabinet as a collection. They are my metaphorical protectors, like brightly colored guard dogs.

Lastly, there is my crucifix collection, displayed in the privacy of my bedroom foyer. They are gathered from my travels as well as given to me by my late grandmothers. These things are very special to me but were more important to honor in the more private areas of my home, due to their spiritual and religious nature.

I remember they were once featured in an article in *The Miami Herald*. The photographer and the writer walked into my bedroom and saw them, and they were compelled to feature them in the story as an influential insight into my personality. It was interesting to see their reaction to a designer's personal collection, which, in the end, made the story more personal and emotional. For me, it brought a sense of reassurance to honor my family history and heritage.

These personal examples can help guide you in deciding where you would like to place your own collections. You can evaluate by asking, "What do I want to show company and what do I want to keep to myself for my own pleasure?"

my crucifx collec-
tion

my Fu Dog
collection

Jars also serve wonderfully to sort things that otherwise would be challenging to display. I had a client that collected shampoo and the soaps from every hotel she went to. What do you do with that? Well, you put them in a jar. This was one of the most sophisticated homes I'd ever worked on, but all of the little plastic shampoo bottles weren't very *beautiful*. I could tell, however, that these were very important to her. I wouldn't dare make her part with them, and so I went and got a jar with a beautiful cover. Voila! Much better!

You can do this with matchsticks or wine corks; there are so many possibilities!

Photography

Today we have Pottery Barn to thank for how beautiful displaying pictures can be. Almost every catalog has a great photo or gallery wall in a perfectly styled display, offering a great example of how you can design with pictures and matted photo frames. There are several specific reasons they look so good. One reason is that the frames are matted, usually with larger-sized mats that enhance the photographs in a neutral color. Secondly, they are usually grouped together closely, no more that three to four inches apart. Lastly, all of the frames are in close harmony with each other by color, size, or texture. Paying close attention to these details will help to create the same effect at home whether purchased all together or gathered over time.

To get started, you will want to revisit all of your photos and see which ones are really meaningful to you. Decide where you want to create your display keeping in mind, as I mentioned earlier, whether they belong in your public or private spaces. Personally, I find that family photos usually look better displayed in the private areas of the home or even in a gallery-like space, such as a staircase or corridor.

Then you can proceed to decide what sizes you want to print them in—small, medium, or large. I consider large to be eight by ten. This is an important distinction, as I wouldn't recommend blowing up pictures into a huge scale unless they're artistic in nature.

An example of artistic means that you might have had your baby photographed by Anne Geddes or something that feels like that. This elevates that photography to the level of art, and it could be big. But if it's just something that was snapped casually and it's not necessarily that creative, then you might want to print it in a smaller scale.

Smaller scale photographs generally looks more sophisticated, especially with a large matt surrounding it, and because people will come up closer to it in order to appreciate it, it makes the interaction even more special for the observer. The smaller it is, the more likely it will be relished upon at close range. When a picture is large, you stand away from it. You want to keep this tip in mind when choosing what to do with your photos and where you will display them.

Grouping and Layering

We've talked about the types of objects you can display and now I want to discuss in greater detail how you can display them.

The first thing is to look at what you have and see how you can put them in a group.

You have your smaller objects, your medium-sized objects, and your larger objects.

The smaller objects could be items such as clocks or figurines. I had a client that collected those little tiny Lalique cut glass animals as tiny as an inch by an inch, which made displaying them very challenging. I suggested a tray to gather them all together. Perfect.

Small items could also be perfume bottles. Usually perfumes are just hanging out on the makeup counter, not necessarily grouped together. This is another perfect tray item. A tray is all you need to take perfumes from cluttered to beautiful.

Books can fall into the small or medium category, especially paperbacks or even smaller ones that becomes difficult to leave out in the open. I've been asked to organize and display other objects like a collection of paper weights, pens—you name it, I've dealt with the challenges of making them look great.

The medium category can be anything from vases and artifacts to sculptures and boxes. The medium-sized objects are also really good to compose together with the smaller and the larger ones.

And then you have some of the larger ones. The larger items that fit into this category are art, larger vases, and even furniture that is not necessarily for use but more artistic in nature.

pause to reflect

CONCLUSION

What a wonderful journey we've just completed! Whether you have implemented every step of the creative process or you are literally still processing, I want to congratulate you for embarking on this journey. I hope that you feel a great deal more aware of your personal *design imprint* and feel empowered to manifest it.

If there is anything that I have complete assuredness of in my life, it is the power that thoughts and ideas have to become a reality. Every day I use my ideas and inspiration to help others create their interior realities. I have literally seen hundreds of projects go from open land and open space to full-blown architectural and interior masterpieces and revel in the glory of creating them. Now it's your turn.

I've shared the tools and a process to use to see the *real you* and how to translate that into your home life as you see fit. I want to once again impart how personal this journey is and how there truly is no wrong and no right.